Contents

THE
PUZZLE
BOOK

THE PUZ

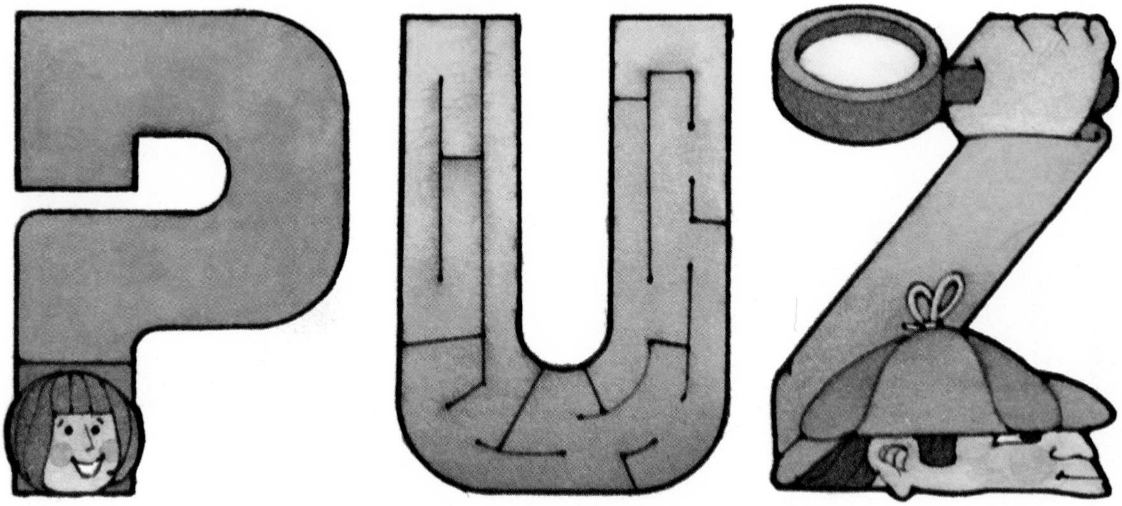

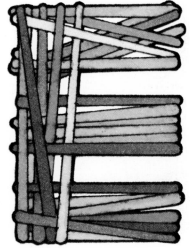

BOOK

The 1982 Childcraft Annual

An annual supplement to
Childcraft – The How and Why Library

World Book, Inc.
a Scott Fetzer company

Chicago London Sydney Toronto

Preface

Everyone loves a puzzle, whether it's a riddle, a tricky question, a "brain teaser," or a code to be solved. Puzzles are fun. They challenge our imagination and make us think.

But, actually, puzzles are more than just a way to have fun. They are also a way of learning *how* to think. It seems that the more puzzles you do, the easier they are to solve. And it seems that as you find it easier to solve puzzles, it is easier for you to solve all kinds of problems!

Puzzles can also help you learn things without even realizing it. One of the world's greatest astronomers has said that he doesn't think mathematics should be taught in schools. He thinks children could learn it more easily by doing puzzles!

So, here's a book full of puzzles of all kinds. If you're like most people, you'll have fun trying to solve them all. And, at the same time, you may learn something. Most of all, though, don't be disappointed if you can't solve a puzzle. Read the answer carefully so you'll see how it was worked out. Then you'll find that the next puzzle may be a little easier.

AND SEEK

In most of these puzzles, you have to look for something that's hidden. It may be a lot of little pictures hidden inside a big one. It may be two things that are just alike, hidden among a lot of things that look different. Or, there may be two things that are different, hidden among a lot of things that look alike. But, whatever it is, the best way to find it is by *looking* very carefully.

Where's Rover?

The children's dog is lost in the middle of the lumberyard! Can you show them which path they have to take to find him?

(answer on page 38)

The last acorn

For weeks, Fletcher
Squirrel has been
gathering acorns.
Now, there is only one
acorn left. Can you
show Fletcher which
branch leads to the
acorn? And remember,
it's not fair to jump
from one branch to
another!

(answer on page 38)

Which balloon?

The little girl has just bought a balloon. The monkey is handing her the string. Which balloon is attached to the string?

(answer on page 38)

Rhyming pairs

On this page there are five pairs of things whose names rhyme. Can you pick out each pair?

(answers on page 39)

1.

A.

2.

B.

3.

C.

4.

D.

5.

E.

Ladybugs, ladybugs!

Which two ladybugs look exactly alike?

(answer on page 39)

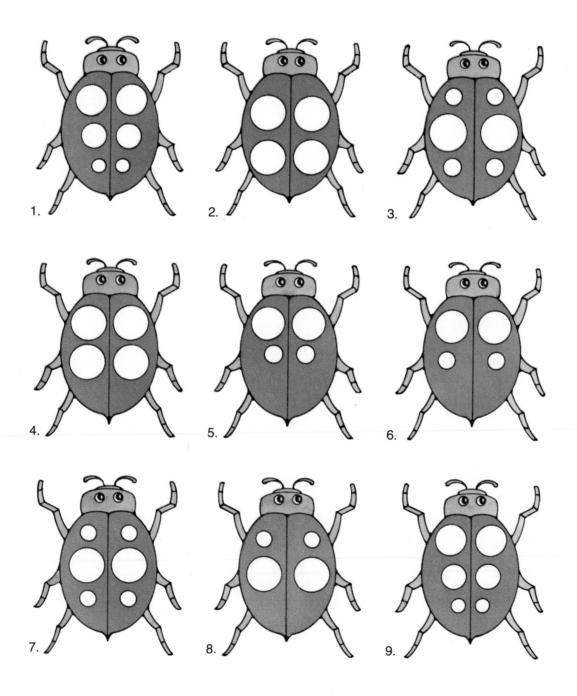

Ollie the Octopus

Which shadow exactly matches Ollie's picture?

(answer on page 39)

1.

2.

3.

4.

5.

6.

What's missing?

The pictures on these two pages seem to be just the same. But if you look closely, you'll see they're not. Some of the things in the

picture on the left-hand page are missing from
the picture on the right-hand page. Can you
find what things are missing?

(answers on page 39)

Finish the picture

Four pieces are missing from this picture. They are mixed up with others, below. Can you find the right pieces and put them where they belong?

(answers on page 40)

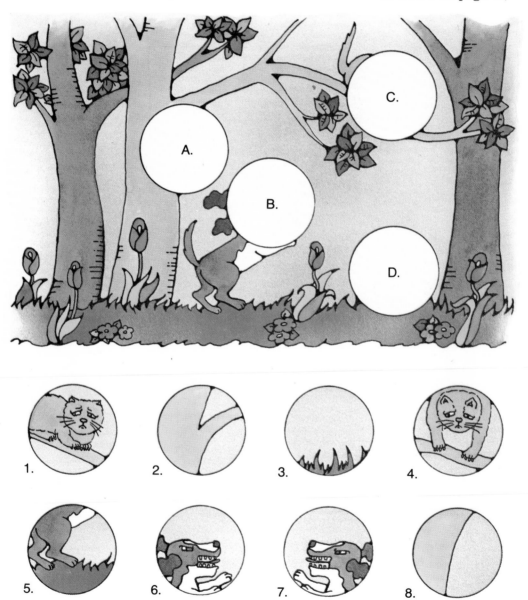

1.

2.

3.

4.

5.

6.

7.

8.

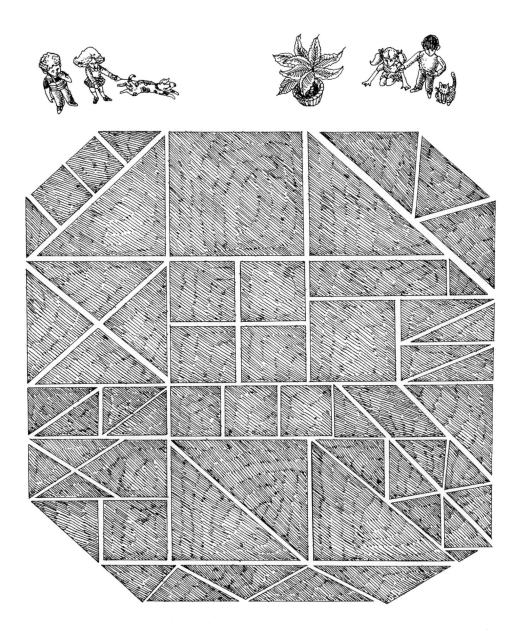

Squares and triangles

Hidden among all the squares and triangles
are three shapes that are *not* squares or
triangles. Can you find them?

(answers on page 40)

Mixed-up snakes

One of these five snakes is different from all
the others. Can you find it?

(answer on page 41)

Lost equipment

A group of children went camping. They lost the nine important things shown at right. The nine things are all hidden somewhere in the picture below. Can you find them?

(answers on page 41)

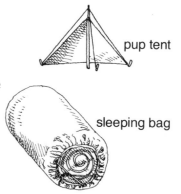

pup tent

sleeping bag

coffee pot

first-aid kit

knapsack

campfire

hiking boot

flashlight

canoe

What's wrong?

There's something wrong with each of these pictures. Do you know what it is?

(answers on page 41)

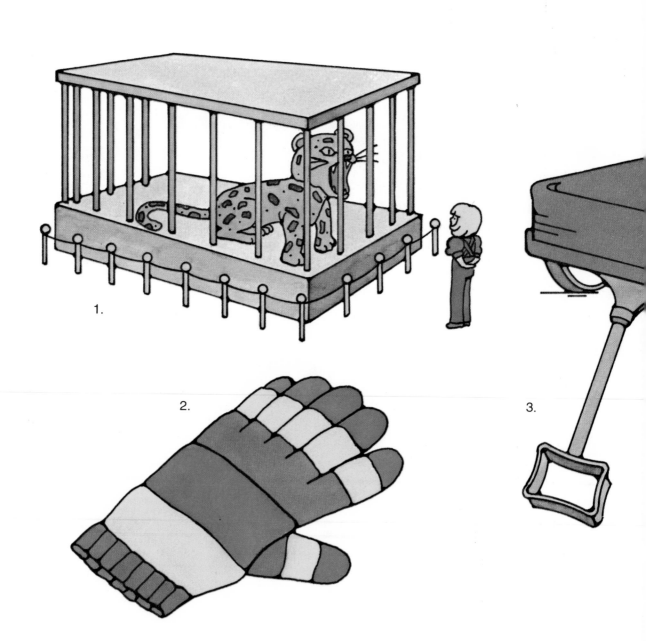

1.

2.

3.

4.

5.

Strange sights!

There are a great many strange things going on in this picture! Can you find them all?

(answers on page 42)

Eye foolers

The things on these pages are all "eye foolers." You may have to look at them in different ways to find the answers.

(answers on page 42)

1. Find the missing piece of pie.

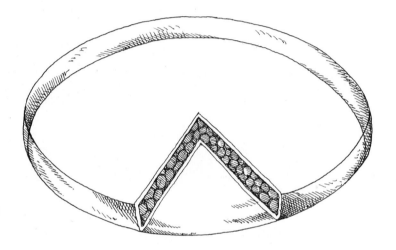

2. Which alligator's eye is closest to the middle alligator's eye?

3. Which elf is the tallest?

4. What does this say?

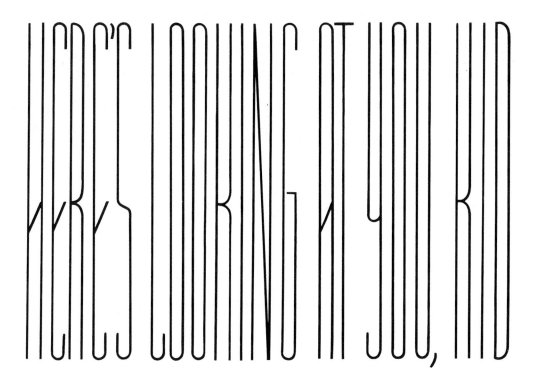

HERE'S LOOKING AT YOU, KID

Picture-words

The first letters in the names of the objects in each row can be put together to make a word. When the three words are put together, they make a sentence. What is the sentence?

(answers on page 42)

Rebus

A rebus is a puzzle in which pictures, letters, and numbers stand for words. In some cases, you must subtract a letter from a word, or from the name of an object, to get the right word. This rebus contains three words that mean a lot to everyone.

(answer on page 42)

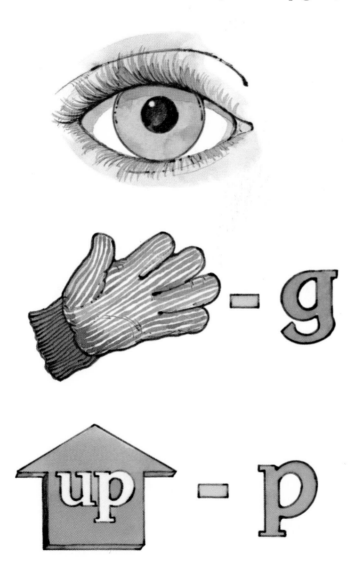

Strange shapes

The picture above shows a desk in an office. There are many objects on the desk. Each object is labeled with a letter. Each picture on the opposite page shows part of each object. Can you match them up? Here's a hint—number 1 is part of E.

(answers on page 43)

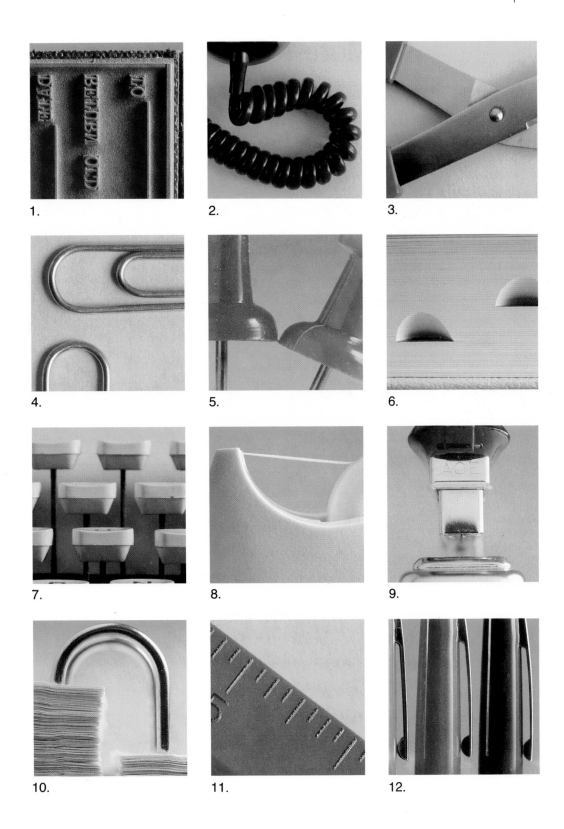

1.

2.

3.

4.

5.

6.

7.

8.

9.

10.

11.

12.

More strange shapes

The pictures below are really nothing more than parts of common, everyday objects. Can you figure out what each one is?

(answers on page 43)

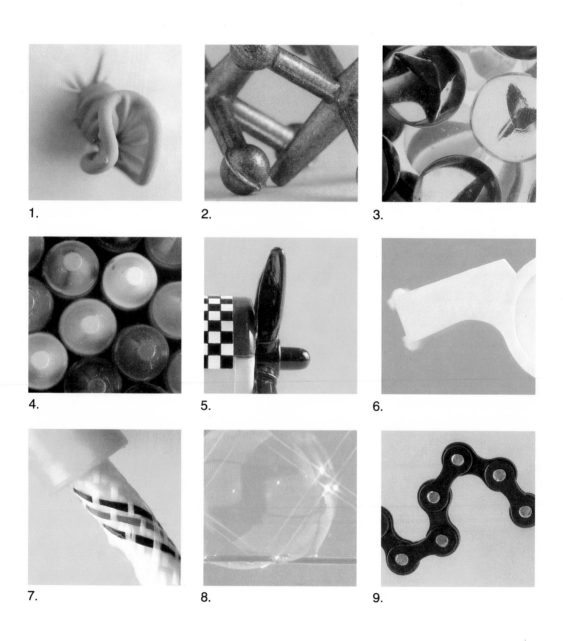

1.

2.

3.

4.

5.

6.

7.

8.

9.

Word pictures

A word picture is a word, or several words, turned into a kind of picture. The picture stands for the name of something. For example,

This word picture is made by splitting the word *banana* in half. And, of course, it stands for—"banana split"!

Now, you try the rest.

(answers on page 43)

1.

2.

3.

4.

5.

6.

7.

8.

Answers

Where's Rover? (page 10)

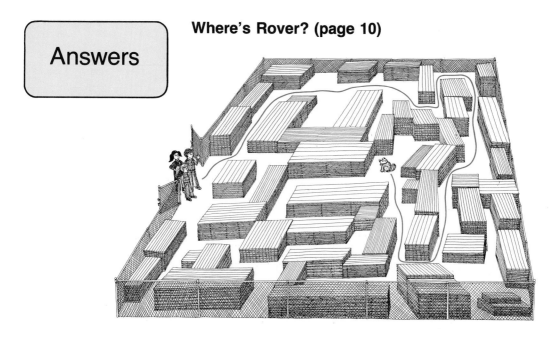

The last acorn (page 12)

Which balloon? (page 14)

Rhyming pairs (page 15)

1—E: goat—boat
2—D: book—cook
3—A: fish—dish
4—B: tree—key
5—C: mouse—house

Answers

Ladybugs, ladybugs! (page 16)

Numbers 1 and 9 are the same.

Ollie the Octopus (page 17)

Ollie's shadow is number 5.

What's missing? (page 18)

The missing things are shown in blue.

Answers

Finish the picture (page 20)

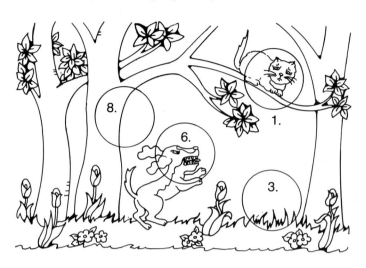

Squares and triangles (page 21)

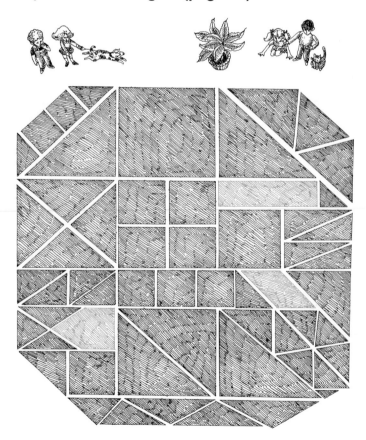

Mixed-up snakes (page 22)

Answers

Lost equipment (page 24)

What's wrong? (page 26)

1. There are no bars on the back of the cage.
2. The glove has six fingers.
3. The body of the wagon is upside down.
4. The pedals are on the back wheel of the bicycle.
5. The grape juice is in the upper part of the glass.

Answers

Strange sights (page 28)

The strange sights are shown in blue.

Eye foolers (page 30)

1. Turn the picture upside down and you'll see the piece of pie.
2. The eyes of both alligators are exactly the same distance from the middle alligator's eye.
3. The elf at the left is the tallest.
4. To read this, hold the edge of the book level with your eyes. If you move the book slightly, you'll see the words. They say: Here's looking at you, kid.

Picture-words (page 32)

*h*elicopter, *o*wl, *w*indmill: how
*a*pple, *r*hinoceros, *e*gg: are
*y*o-yo, *o*strich, *u*mbrella: you

Rebus (page 33)

I love you

Strange shapes (page 34)

1—E: rubber stamp
2—D: telephone cord
3—I: scissors
4—L: paper clips
5—F: pushpins
6—G: edge of book
7—J: typewriter keys
8—C: transparent tape and dispenser
9—B: stapler
10—A: desk calendar
11—H: ruler
12—K: pen

More strange shapes (page 36)

1. tied end of balloon
2. jacks
3. marbles
4. crayons
5. model airplane propeller
6. mouth of whistle
7. bottom of jump rope and handle
8. soap bubble and bubble ring
9. bicycle chain

Word pictures (page 37)

1. jump rope
2. sidewalk
3. running in a circle
4. hide and seek
5. breakfast
6. crosseye
7. upside-down cake
8. a long time ago

Riddles are probably the very oldest kind of puzzle. People have been making up riddles and having fun solving them for thousands of years. And some riddles that are thousands of years old are still known to this day.

In olden times, people often used riddles to teach children about many of the things they needed to know. Solving riddles is also a way of learning how to solve different kinds of problems. You'll find that these riddles will help you get "warmed up" for solving the "Brain Teasers" and some of the other kinds of puzzles in this book.

Riddles from long ago

Most of these riddles are hundreds of years old. The first one is more than two thousand years old!

What creature walks on four legs in the morning, two legs in the afternoon, and three legs in the evening?

A person. As a baby, in the *morning* of life, a person crawls on all fours. As a grown-up, in the *noontime* of life, a person walks on two legs. As an old man or woman, in the *evening* of life, a person often needs a cane to help him walk.

Runs all day, but never walks;
Often murmurs, but never talks;
It has a bed, but never sleeps;
It has a mouth but never eats.

A river.

What flies forever and rests never?

The wind.

In spring I look gay,
Dressed in bright array.
In summer more clothing I wear.
But when colder it grows,
I fling off my clothes,
And in winter quite naked appear.
What am I?

A tree.

The more you feed it,
The more it will grow high.
But if you give it water,
Then it will simply die.
What is it?

Fire.

There may be a houseful or a holeful,
But you cannot catch a bowlful.
What is it?

Smoke.

What kind of water never freezes?

Hot water.

What grows bigger
the more you take from it?

A hole in the ground.

A box without hinges, a key, or lid,
Yet, golden treasure inside is hid.
What is it?

An egg.

What grows with its roots upward in
winter and cannot grow in summer?

An icicle.

What has teeth but cannot bite?

A comb.

Alive without breath;
As cold as death.
Never thirsty, ever drinking;
All in mail never clinking.
What is it?

A fish.

What has an eye
but cannot see?

A needle.

The King of Cumberland
Gave the Queen of Northumberland
A bottomless container
To put flesh and blood in.
What was it?

A ring for her finger.

Riddles from many lands

These are some of the favorite riddles of
children from many different countries. You
may be surprised to find that some of these
riddles are like the ones that you know.

Brazil

A crowd of girls dressed in yellow
are peeking out of a grocery store.
What are they?

A bunch of bananas.

Canada

It's as green as grass.
It's as black as coal.
Along comes a hungry soul
And puts it into a red hole.
What is it?

A blackberry.

Norway

What is the strongest animal of all?

The snail. It carries its house around.

Germany

Why did Hannibal cross the Alps?

He wanted to get to the other side.

Italy

Why did General Garibaldi wear red, white, and green suspenders to the Battle of Calatafimi?

To hold his pants up.

Israel

I'm not an airplane,
but I fly through the sky.
I'm not a river,
but I'm full of water.
What am I?

A cloud.

Africa (Kxatla people)

A white horse goes into the stable and comes out brown. *What is it?*

A loaf of bread. The dough is white when it goes into the oven (stable), and comes out brown when it is baked.

Russia

What kind of a bush
does a fox sit under
during a rainstorm?

A wet one.

China

What is it that is made
dirty by washing?

Water.

India

Who never speaks until he is slapped,
then cries out in a deep voice?

A drum.

Egypt

Why does a pelican stand
with one leg off the ground?

Because it would fall down if it tried
to stand with both legs off the ground.

England

It's in rock but not in stone,
It's in marrow but not in bone,
It's in a bolster but not in a bed,
It's not in the live and not in the dead.
What is it?

The letter r.

France

Which is heavier, a pound of feathers
or a pound of lead?

They both weigh the same. A pound
is a pound no matter what it's made of.

Ireland

A white barn with two roofs
and no door at all, at all.
What is it?

An egg.

Japan

What has six legs but walks on only four?

A man on a horse.

Mexico

Why is a guitar like a comb?

> Neither one of them
> can climb a tree.

Poland

What does a pig have that even
a king doesn't have?

> An owner.

Puerto Rico

I come from San Juan, talking like a priest.
I have a little green body and a red heart on my chest.
What am I?

> A parrot.

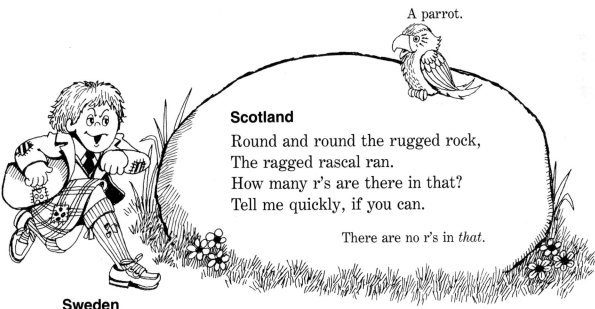

Scotland

Round and round the rugged rock,
The ragged rascal ran.
How many r's are there in that?
Tell me quickly, if you can.

> There are no r's in *that*.

Sweden

What travels in all directions,
yet is never on the ground or in the air?

> A fish.

Joke riddles

The answers to these riddles really don't make much sense. But they're funny!

GENUINE FUR

Why does a bear have a fur coat?

Because it would look silly in a raincoat.

Name six things that have milk in them.

Ice cream, cocoa, pudding, and three cows.

What has a hundred legs, but can't walk a single step?

Fifty pairs of pants.

Why was the little boy surprised
to find celery growing out of his ears?

Because he had planted carrots.

Which is faster, heat or cold?

Heat, because you can catch cold.

What time is it if a grandfather clock
strikes thirteen times?

Time to get the clock fixed!

A coffin maker was making a coffin. But
every time he tried to hammer a nail into
it, it slid away from him. He had to keep
chasing it around the workshop! How could
he stop the coffin?

He should give it a cough drop.
That usually stops coffin.

Why were ancient Egyptian boys
and girls such good children?

Because they respected their mummies.

Why did the little girl walk home instead of taking a bus?

Because she knew that if she took a bus, her mother would make her put it back.

What bus once crossed an ocean?

Colum-bus

What's the longest word in the dictionary?

Smile—there's a mile after the first letter.

Why did the little boy take a ruler to bed with him?

Because he wanted to find out how long he was asleep.

A little girl was locked in a room with no windows. The room was empty except for a grand piano. How did she get out of the locked room?

She found the right key on the piano.

A man was taking a bucket of glue, a roll of wrapping paper, a sponge, and some nails to work. He got caught in a rainstorm and went into an old, empty house. The man was nervous because the house was supposed to be haunted. Suddenly, he heard a rapping sound! What do you think was making the rapping?

The wrapping paper.

How long should a ten-year-old boy's legs be?

Just long enough to reach the ground.

What would happen if you swallowed a soup spoon?

You soon wouldn't be able to stir.

What do elephants have that no other kind of animal in the world has?

Baby elephants.

As a man walked down a street, three beggars asked him for money, one after another. He gave each one twenty-five cents. What time was it?

A quarter-to-three.

Why did the little girl think that the cook
was mean?

She saw him beating eggs and whipping cream.

Why was the little raspberry crying?

Because its mom and dad were in a jam.

Why do birds fly south for the winter?

Because it's too far to walk.

Why isn't it a good idea to go for a walk
on an empty stomach?

Because it's easier to walk on a sidewalk.

What does an envelope say when it's licked?

It just shuts up and doesn't say anything.

What animal can jump higher than
a mountain?

Any animal. A mountain can't jump!

What's the difference between an elephant
and a flea?

An elephant can have fleas, but a flea
can't have elephants.

TEASERS

These puzzles are real foolers. They are not quite what they seem to be. They're intended to show you that what may seem to be a difficult problem often has an easy answer. In fact, the answer may be "right under your nose."

So, here's a hint for doing these puzzles. Don't look for a complicated answer. The answer is usually very simple, and is hidden in what the puzzle says.

Three into twelve

There are twelve one-cent stamps in a dozen. How many three-cent stamps are in a dozen?

(answer on page 91)

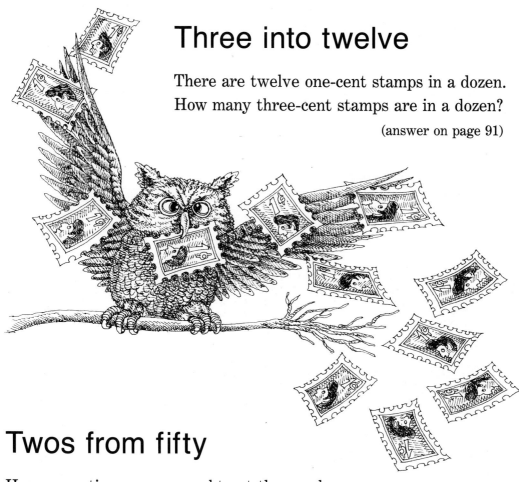

Twos from fifty

How many times can you subtract the number two from the number fifty?

(answer on page 91)

The Rabbit family

Mr. and Mrs. Bixley Rabbit have six children who are boy rabbits. Each boy rabbit has two sisters. How many children are there in the Rabbit family?

(answer on page 91)

Mr. Chugginmugger's eggs

Every morning, it takes Mr. Finster Chugginmugger three minutes to boil an egg for his breakfast. One day, two friends joined him for breakfast. How long will it take him to boil three eggs?

(answer on page 91)

Mr. Wu's Watch

One morning, a light bulb in a ceiling fixture at Mr. Wu's Chinese restaurant burned out. Mr. Wu climbed up on a stepladder to change the bulb. As he was standing on the ladder, his watch fell out of his pocket. It went right into a large bowl of tea! But when Mr. Wu climbed down and took his watch out of the tea, it wasn't the least bit wet. Why not?

(answer on page 91)

Dime disappointment

A boy named Robert collected old coins. He knew that some old coins were worth a lot of money. But he didn't know if any of his coins were valuable.

One day, his friend Susan told him she had heard that 1950 dimes (ten-cent pieces) were worth almost two hundred dollars. Robert looked at his coins. He had two 1950 dimes!

He rushed to the bank to turn in the two coins and collect almost four hundred dollars. However, at the bank he was told that while 1950 dimes were worth almost two hundred dollars, his two dimes were worth only twenty cents. Why?

(answer on page 91)

The mysterious tunnel

Not far outside the town of Pottsville, a railroad track runs through a tunnel in a hillside. There is only one track, and the tunnel is wide enough for only one train. But one day, two trains went into the tunnel from opposite directions. Each train entered the tunnel at exactly eight o'clock. Three minutes later, each train came out at the opposite end of the tunnel. Yet there was no collision! How was this possible?

(answer on page 92)

The scientist's brother

Mr. Smith proudly told everyone that he is the brother of a famous scientist. However, Mr. Smith doesn't *have* a brother. Even so, he was telling the truth! How was this possible?

(answer on page 92)

The bus driver

A bus driver was going down a street. He went right past a stop sign without stopping. He turned left where there was a "no left turn" sign. Then he turned the wrong way into a one-way street. And yet, he didn't break a single traffic law. Why not?

(answer on page 92)

The sun and the mountain

When it is noon at a certain place on the earth's equator, or middle, there is a mountain that is almost eight thousand miles (12,800 kilometers) closer to the sun than it is at midnight. Why is this?

(answer on page 92)

The wizard's problem

The old wizard of Wallapoo lived alone in a tall tower on a hilltop. One day, he decided to take a bath.

The bathroom was at the very top of the tower. It was a small room, with only one door and no windows. The walls, floor, and ceiling were made of stone.

The wizard got into the tub and turned on the water. Just then, his cat chased a mouse past the door. The cat bumped into the door and it swung shut with a thump. The bump jarred the latch, and the wizard heard it click. He was locked in the bathroom!

Angrily, the wizard turned off the faucet—and the handle broke off in his hand. Water continued to pour out of the faucet. There was no way to shut it off. Slowly, the water began to fill the bathtub. The wizard knew that in time the whole room would be filled with water—and he couldn't get out!

How did the wizard keep from drowning? (He *didn't* use magic.)

(answer on page 92)

Which way to Smidgin-on-Syme?

Long ago, a minstrel walked down a country road. He had just come from a little town called Puddly-by-the-Marsh. He had made quite a bit of money there, entertaining at a wedding. Now he was on his way to the town of Smidgin-on-Syme. A rich baron who lived there would pay him well for entertaining at banquets. The minstrel had been warned not to go through a town called Blugsby, for robbers attacked people who went that way.

After a time, the minstrel came to a fork in the road. He could go left or right. One road went straight to Smidgin-on-Syme. The other road went through Blugsby. But the minstrel didn't know which road to take. And the signpost, with its three signs pointing to three different towns had been blown down by a storm. It lay by the road, and there was no way to tell which way each sign had pointed.

The minstrel thought for a moment. Then he saw how he could find the road that went to Smidgin-on-Syme. How did he do it?

(answer on page 92)

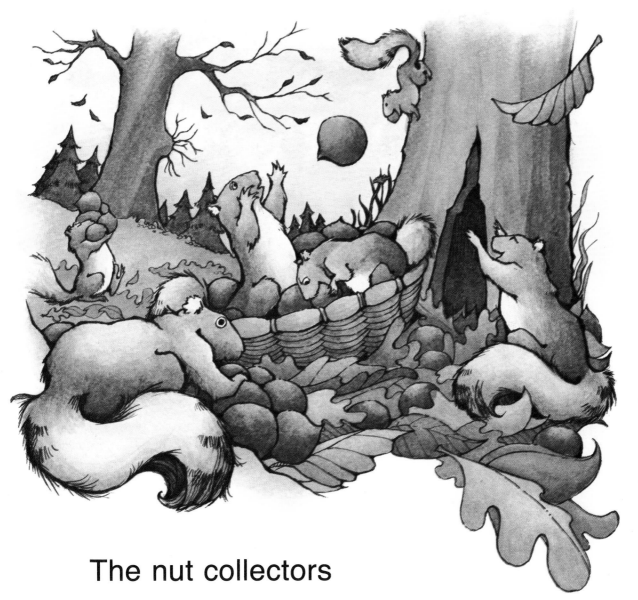

The nut collectors

Six squirrels began to gather hickory nuts and put them into a large basket. The squirrels worked so fast that the number of nuts in the basket was doubled at the end of every minute. The basket was completely full at the end of ten minutes. How many minutes had it taken the squirrels to get the basket half full?

(answer on page 93)

A sailor's puzzle

Long ago, a ship was anchored in the port of Amsterdam. A rope ladder hung over the ship's side. There were sixteen rungs in the ladder. The bottom rung of the ladder just touched the water.

Every half hour, the tide rose exactly one-half the distance between two rungs of the ladder. How long did it take for the water to cover four rungs of the ladder?

(answer on page 93)

A rainy day mystery

A brother and sister were waiting for the school bus. The morning had been bright and sunny, but now the sky started to cloud over. There was a sprinkle of rain, then a shower, then a cloudburst. The rain lasted for five minutes. The children had no umbrellas or raincoats, and there was no shelter where the bus stopped. But when the bus came, a few minutes after the rain stopped, the two children were perfectly dry. How was this possible?

(answer on page 93)

The speechless parrot

A man bought a parrot at a pet shop. The owner of the pet shop guaranteed that the parrot could repeat any word it heard. The man took the parrot home, but it never spoke a single word. Nevertheless, what the pet shop owner had said was absolutely true—the parrot *could* repeat any word it heard. So, why didn't it talk?

(answer on page 93)

The prisoner

Pietro, the brave young leader of the rebels, had been captured by the soldiers of the wicked Duke Malvolio. They took him to the castle and put him into the dungeon.

"Tomorrow morning, the Duke will have you hanged," said the captain of the soldiers. Then, grinning wickedly, he slammed the heavy wooden door and locked it.

Young Pietro looked around the empty cell. It was square, with walls and ceiling made of stone. The floor was bare earth. In one wall there was a narrow window. Pietro thought he could squeeze through the window if he could reach it. But it was so high up that he couldn't reach it even by jumping.

Pietro was in despair. Tomorrow he was to die, and there seemed no way to escape!

Suddenly, he threw himself down on the floor and began to dig in the dirt with his hands. He had thought of a way to escape through the window by digging a hole in the floor! Do you know what he planned to do?

(answer on page 93)

The amazing rabbit

Two rabbits were nibbling clover in a meadow. They were facing in opposite directions. Suddenly, one cried out to the other: "Look out! There's a fox sneaking up behind you!"

The rabbit didn't hear or smell the fox. How did it know the fox was sneaking up behind its friend?

(answer on page 94)

How did he know?

A man was waiting at an airport for a plane to arrive. Suddenly, he heard someone call his name. Looking up, he saw an old friend of his hurrying toward him.

"Hey, Bill!" called his friend. "How are you? I haven't seen you in years!"

"How are *you?*" exclaimed Bill. "Wow, you look great!"

"I'm married now, to somebody you don't know," said the other. "This is my daughter."

Bill smiled down at the little girl. "Hi, young lady. What's your name?"

"It's the same as my mama's," said the girl. "Is that so," said Bill, winking at his friend. "Then your name must be Cindy!"

How could he possibly know this?

(answer on page 94)

The stuck truck

A large truck was stuck in an underpass. The underpass was exactly as high as the truck. When the driver had tried to get through, the truck had become wedged tight. It couldn't go backward or forward. Traffic was piling up behind it.

Then, a little boy walked up to the truckdriver and made a suggestion. In a few minutes, the truck was no longer stuck in the underpass. What did the boy tell the driver?

(answer on page 94)

Hungry horses

If five horses can eat five bags of oats in five minutes, how long will it take a hundred horses to eat a hundred bags of oats?

(answer on page 94)

The dirty trick

Two boys, named Ralph and Simon, were fishing from the edge of a little stream. It was a warm, sunny day, and before long both boys fell asleep.

Ralph's sister, Marilyn, happened by and saw the sleeping boys. For a joke, she very gently smeared each boy's face with mud.

A few minutes later, both boys woke up. At the sight of Ralph's muddy face, Simon burst into laughter. Seeing Simon's muddy face, Ralph also began to laugh.

Suddenly, Simon stopped laughing. He quickly scooped up some water and washed his face. Neither boy had said a word, and Simon couldn't see himself. How did he know his face was dirty?

(answer on page 94)

An underwater stunt

Sam and Beth were standing at the edge of the swimming pool.

"I can hold my breath for a whole minute," Sam told Beth. "Watch me. I'll stay underwater for one minute."

He dived into the pool. Beth looked at her wristwatch. Sure enough, Sam stayed underwater for just about one minute.

"That's nothing," said Beth. "*I* can stay underwater for *five* minutes!"

"That's impossible!" scoffed Sam. "No one can hold their breath that long."

"I bet I can stay underwater for five minutes," Beth repeated. So Sam bet her.

Beth won the bet. How did she do it?

(answer on page 94)

The museum

Professor Priscilla Pippen was a history teacher at a college. One Saturday as she drove through a very small town, she saw a tiny building with a sign on it. The sign read, "Museum of Natural History." Professor Pippen parked her car and went into the museum.

There were only five exhibits in the museum. These were:

1. A prehistoric arrowhead made of copper.

2. The fossil skeleton of a dinosaur no bigger than a chicken.

3. An ancient Roman coin marked with the date 120 B.C.

4. A red diamond in a ring.

5. An ancient Egyptian cat mummy.

Professor Pippen knew at once that one of the exhibits was a fake. Which one was it?

(answer on page 95)

Leftover sandwiches

Mrs. Martin made twenty-four sandwiches for
a picnic. All but seven were eaten. How many
were left?

(answer on page 95)

Even money

Two mothers and two daughters decided to go
shopping. They found that they had
twenty-seven dollars, all in one-dollar bills.
They divided up the money evenly, without
making any of the dollars into change, so that
they each had exactly the same amount. How
was this possible?

(answer on page 95)

An elevator puzzle

Tom lives on the fifteenth floor—the very top floor—of a tall building in a large city. There are stairs connecting each floor of the building. But, of course, most people usually use the elevator to get up and down.

In the elevator, the buttons for the floors are in one row, going from top to bottom. The button for the first floor is at the bottom. Thus, when Tom wants to go down to the ground floor, he presses the lowest button.

When Tom takes the elevator up, he always rides all the way to the fifteenth floor if there are other people on the elevator. But if he is alone, he always presses the button for the tenth floor. He gets off on the tenth floor and walks up five flights of stairs to the fifteenth floor.

Tom would rather ride the elevator all the way to the fifteenth floor. But he never does when he is alone. Why not?

(answer on page 95)

A windy day puzzle

It was a windy day in autumn. Most of the leaves had been blown off the trees. The Johnsons' lawn was covered with red, yellow, and brown leaves.

Randy Johnson came out to rake the leaves for his parents. Just for fun, he first raked the leaves into small piles. He made six piles in one corner of the lawn, and half as many piles in another corner. In a third corner there were twice as many piles, and in the fourth corner only a third as many piles.

Randy then began to rake all the leaves into one pile in the middle of the lawn. Just then a gust of wind blew into one of the piles. It picked up all the leaves in the pile and scattered them over the neighborhood! How many piles did Randy finally end up with?

(answer on page 96)

The mystery of the missing fish

Two fathers and two sons went fishing. Each caught one fish. However, only three fish were caught. How was this possible?

(answer on page 96)

The tennis player

Once there was a player
In a tennis game.
She played very well,
And won great fame.
Jane was her first name,
What was her last name.

The tennis player's last name is hidden in the poem. Can you find it?

(answer on page 96)

The hungry Vikings

Long ago, a band of Vikings, with their wives
and children, made ready for a long journey.
They would sail from Norway to Iceland, to
make new homes.

They would be at sea for weeks, living on
hard crackers and dried, cold meat. They
couldn't cook aboard ship for fear of fire. They
all knew they'd be yearning for a good meal of
roast pork when they finally reached land.
But any pork they took along would spoil long
before they got to Iceland.

Rolf Hairybeard, the Viking chieftain,
talked over the problem with some of his men.

"We could tie long ropes to big pieces of
meat and let them trail in the water,"

suggested one man. "That might keep them cool enough so they wouldn't spoil."

"Sharks would eat the meat," Hairybeard pointed out.

"Let's keep the meat aboard ship, but pile up snow and ice around it to keep it cold," said another of the Vikings.

"The ship would get full of water when the ice and snow melted," objected Hairybeard.

"I can tell you how to keep meat fresh for as long as you want," said Hairybeard's wife, Gunnhilda. When she told the men her idea, they all agreed it would work. What was her idea?

(answer on page 96)

The fake inventor

For many years, chemists have tried to invent a "universal" solvent—a substance that will dissolve anything. Such a substance would be worth a fortune.

One day, not long ago, a man asked to see the president of a large chemical company. "I have invented the universal solvent," the man said proudly. He held up a small bottle filled with greenish liquid. "I have it right here. I'll sell you the formula for only ten thousand dollars!"

"You're a fake," said the chemical company president. "Get out of here!"

Why did he say the man was a fake when he hadn't even tested the liquid?

(answer on page 97)

A cutting problem

1. You have five pieces of chain. There are three links in each piece.

   To fasten two pieces together, you would have to cut a link apart, join it to another link, then close it up.

   How many links would you have to cut apart in order to join all five pieces to make one chain?

   (answer on page 97)

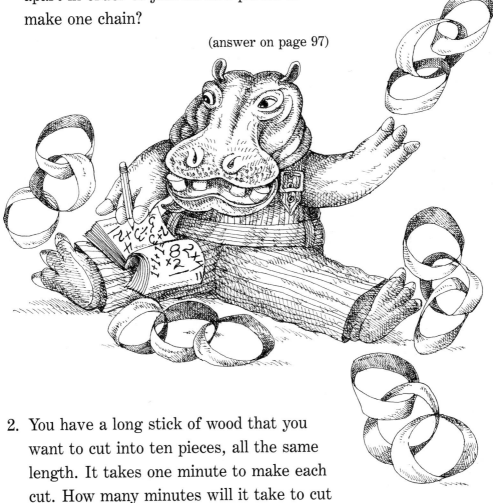

2. You have a long stick of wood that you want to cut into ten pieces, all the same length. It takes one minute to make each cut. How many minutes will it take to cut the stick into the ten pieces?

   (answer on page 97)

The strange sisters

It was the first day of school. The teacher had several new children in her class. She asked all the new children to write down their names and their date of birth for her.

The first two names she looked at were those of girls. She saw that they both had the same last name. They also had the same birthday—June 9, 1973. "Will Jane and June Campbell please stand?" asked the teacher.

Two girls stood up, and the teacher saw that they looked just alike. "Oh, you're twins," she said.

One of the girls shook her head. "No," she said. "We're sisters, but we're not twins."

How could they be sisters and be the same age, but not be twins?

(answer on page 97)

Three into twelve (page 62)

There are twelve three-cent stamps in a dozen, just as there are twelve one-cent stamps in a dozen. A dozen is twelve of anything.

Twos from fifty (page 62)

You can subtract two from fifty only *once*. After that, the fifty is forty-eight.

The Rabbit family (page 62)

There are eight children in the Rabbit family—six boy rabbits and two girl rabbits. Each boy rabbit has two sisters, but they're the *same* two.

Mr. Chugginmugger's eggs (page 63)

If Mr. Chugginmugger has two guests for breakfast, he will boil their eggs at the same time he boils his own. One egg will boil in three minutes, then three eggs in the same pot will also boil in three minutes.

Mr. Wu's watch (page 64)

The watch fell into a bowl containing dry tea leaves.

Dime disappointment (page 65)

If you add up 1950 dimes—that is, one thousand, nine hundred and fifty dimes—you'll find they amount to $195.00, which is almost two hundred dollars, as the girl told Robert. However, a dime with the year 1950 on it is worth only ten cents, like most other dimes.

Answers

The mysterious tunnel (page 66)

One train went through the tunnel at eight o'clock in the morning. The other train went through at eight o'clock at night.

The scientist's brother (page 67)

The famous scientist was a woman. She was Mr. Smith's sister.

The bus driver (page 67)

The bus driver didn't break any traffic laws because it was his day off and he was walking.

The sun and the mountain (page 67)

At noon, the mountain faces the sun. During the rest of the day, as the earth rotates, or turns, the mountain moves away from the sun. By midnight, the earth has turned halfway around. The whole earth is then *between* the mountain and the sun. The earth is almost eight thousand miles (12,800 kilometers) thick at the equator, so the mountain is that much farther away from the sun than it is at noon.

The wizard's problem (page 68)

To keep from drowning all the wizard had to do was pull out the plug in the bathtub! But then he had to figure out how to open the door. And that was a lot harder!

Which way to Smidgin-on-Syme (page 70)

The minstrel knew the name of the town he had just come from—Puddly-by-the-Marsh. All he had to do was put the signpost back up with the Puddly-by-the-Marsh sign pointing back toward the way he had come. Then the other signs would point in the right directions.

The nut collectors (page 71)

If the number of nuts in the basket doubled at the end of every minute, the basket must have been half full in nine minutes. Then, after one more minute, the half would be doubled, thus filling the other half of the basket.

A sailor's puzzle (page 72)

The water never covered any of the rungs. A ship, of course, floats on water. So, as the tide rose, the ship rose with it. And the rope ladder, which was attached to the ship, also rose.

A rainy day mystery (page 73)

The children were inside their house while they waited for the bus.

The speechless parrot (page 73)

The parrot couldn't hear any words to repeat. It was deaf.

The prisoner (page 74)

By digging a deep hole in the floor of the cell, Pietro could make a large pile of dirt. Then, by standing on the pile of dirt, he could reach the window.

Answers

The amazing rabbit (page 76)

Although the rabbits were facing in opposite directions, they were facing each other. Thus, the rabbit could *see* the fox sneaking toward his friend.

How did he know? (page 76)

Bill knew the little girl's name because it was the same as his friend's name. His old friend, to whom he was talking, was named Cindy, and she was the little girl's mother.

The stuck truck (page 77)

The boy suggested that the driver let some air out of each of the tires. This lowered the truck just enough so that it no longer pressed against the top of the underpass.

Hungry horses (page 77)

If five horses can eat five bags of oats in five minutes, then it takes *each* horse five minutes to eat a bag of oats. Therefore, it will take only five minutes for a hundred horses to eat a hundred bags of oats.

The dirty trick (page 78)

Simon was laughing at Ralph because Ralph's face was dirty. When he saw that Ralph was laughing at him, he realized his face must be dirty, too.

An underwater stunt (page 79)

Beth filled a cup with water. Then she held the cup over her head for five minutes.

The museum (page 81)

The fake exhibit was number 3—the ancient Roman coin marked 120 B.C. The abbreviation B.C. stands for "Before Christ." People who lived 120 years before Christ couldn't possibly have known it, of course! So they would not have put B.C. on any of their coins.

Leftover sandwiches (page 82)

If all but seven sandwiches were eaten, then seven sandwiches were left, of course.

Even money (page 82)

The two mothers and two daughters were actually only three people—Sue, her mother, and her grandmother. Sue was her mother's daughter, of course, and her mother was the grandmother's daughter—that's two daughters. Sue's mother was one mother, and *her* mother, the grandmother, was the other mother. Thus, they divided the twenty-seven dollars three ways, each taking nine dollars.

An elevator puzzle (page 83)

Tom is a small, six-year-old boy. He can easily reach the lowest button when he wants to go down to the first floor. But when he wants to go up, and he is alone, he has a problem. He can't reach the top button, which is for the fifteenth floor. He can reach only as high as the tenth button. So, he has to get off at the tenth floor and walk up to the fifteenth floor.

However, if other people are in the elevator, he asks someone to press the top button for him.

Answers

A windy day puzzle (page 84)

After the gust of wind blew away one of the piles, Randy continued to rake the leaves into one pile in the middle of the lawn. So, of course, he *ended up* with only one pile.

The mystery of the missing fish (page 85)

The two fathers and two sons who went fishing were actually only three people—a grandfather, his son, and his grandson. The grandfather was his son's father, of course, and the son was the grandson's father. That makes two fathers. The grandfather's son was one son, and *his* son was the other. So, if each of them caught one fish, only three fish were caught.

The tennis player (page 85)

The tennis player's first *and* last names are given in the last two lines of the poem.

Jane was her first name,
What was her last name.

The two lines make one complete sentence. And there is a period at the end of the sentence, *not* a question mark. So the sentence *tells* something, it doesn't ask a question. It tells you that *Jane* was the player's first name and that *What* was her last name. Her name was Jane What.

The hungry Vikings (page 86)

Gunnhilda's idea was to keep some live pigs in a cage on the ship. When the Vikings got to Iceland, they could butcher the animals and have fresh meat for a feast.

The fake inventor (page 88)

If the liquid could truly dissolve anything, as the inventor claimed, it would have dissolved the glass bottle it was in.

Answers

A cutting problem (page 89)

1. To join all five pieces of chain to make one single chain, you have to cut only the *three* links of one piece. With those three links you can link the other pieces together, as shown.

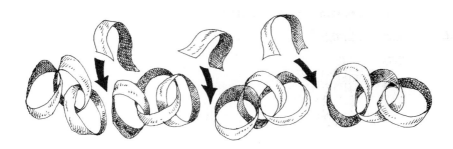

2. It will take you *nine* minutes to cut the stick into ten pieces, because you need to make only nine cuts. The ninth cut turns the last section of wood into two pieces—the ninth and tenth pieces.

The strange sisters (page 90)

Jane and June Campbell were sisters, and they were born on the same day in the the same year. But they weren't twins. They were two of a set of triplets. The other triplet, a boy, was in the class, too.

A mystery story is a kind of puzzle. Many people think it's the very best kind of puzzle. They enjoy trying to find the clues and then put them together to solve the crime.

So, if you're the kind of person who likes to play detective, here's a short mystery story. It takes place at night, in a big, old house, during a thunderstorm. The story is filled with clues. If you spot them, you can figure out who committed the crime.

The Mystery of the Chinese Vase

It was one minute after eleven o'clock at night. A torrent of rain poured down out of a pitch-black sky. It drummed on the roof of the big, old house that sat in the middle of a huge yard surrounded by a high iron fence. Two lights burned in rooms on the second floor. Several others glowed on the first floor.

Suddenly, the sky was shattered by a titanic crash of thunder. An instant later, a girl screamed, "Mr. Potney! Mr. Potney!"

On the second floor of the house, a door opened. A young man in pajamas, his hair all mussed and his eyes blinking sleepily, peered out. At the far end of the long hall, a light shone through the doorway of another room. A young woman stood there. When she saw the young man, she came running toward him.

"Jack! Jack!" she cried.

"Elaine, what's the matter?" he asked. "I

was asleep, but I thought I heard someone call out. What's happened?"

"Oh, Jack, your uncle has been robbed," the girl exclaimed. "His Chinese vase has been stolen!"

Just then, a door opened in the middle of the hall. An elderly man, clad in bathrobe and slippers, stepped out.

"Did someone call me?" he asked. "I was taking a shower and couldn't hear well."

"Elaine says your Chinese vase has been stolen, Uncle Henry," exclaimed Jack.

"Yes, Mr. Potney," the girl sobbed.

"Good heavens!" gasped Mr. Potney. He ran up the hall toward his bedroom. Jack and Elaine hurried after him.

Against one bedroom wall stood a large wooden cabinet in which Mr. Potney kept his Chinese vase. The vase was hundreds of years old—and worth thousands of dollars.

The cabinet was always closed and locked. But now, the cabinet door was wide open and the vase was gone!

"Someone pried the door open!" Mr. Potney exclaimed. He looked at the girl. "How did you find out about this, Elaine?"

"I was downstairs watching television until just a few minutes ago," said Elaine. "When I came upstairs, the door to your room was open. I knew you were taking a shower, so I wondered why the light was on. I looked in and saw the open cabinet. The vase was gone. That's when I called you."

Jack looked at Elaine rather suspiciously. She was his uncle's private secretary, and Jack liked her. But he wondered if she were telling the truth. She could have taken the vase!

Jack's feet were bare, and he suddenly realized that the rug felt damp. Could rain have blown into the room? Maybe the thief had come in through a window and left it open.

Jack looked about. No, all the windows were closed. Then a gleam caught his eye. Lying in a corner of the room was a small kitchen knife. He pointed to it. "Look! I'll bet that's what was used to pry open the cabinet."

Mr. Potney started to pick up the knife, but Jack stopped him. "There may be fingerprints on it, Uncle Henry. We should call the police."

He hurried out of the room and headed for the stairs, the others after him. The stairs were carpeted, and several times Jack thought he felt dampness on his bare feet.

As Jack and the others reached the foot of the stairs, three people came hurrying toward them. One was chubby Mrs. Elson, the cook. Behind her were tall, thin Julian, the chauffeur, and sturdy Mr. Stokes, the butler. Mrs. Elson and Julian were fully dressed. Stokes was in pajamas, bathrobe, and slippers. But, of course, his gray hair was neatly combed. Stokes always managed to look well-groomed.

"We heard someone call out," panted Mrs. Elson. "Is there a fire?"

Jack stared at her for a moment. He knew that the knife that had been used to pry open the cabinet was one of the knives she used in

the kitchen. Could she be the thief? "My uncle's priceless Chinese vase has been stolen," he told her.

Mrs. Elson gasped, and looked as if she were going to faint. While the others fussed over her, Jack walked into the next room. This was the room in which Elaine said she had been watching television. He put his hand on the television set. It was still warm. The set had certainly been on until only a short time ago, but that didn't prove that Elaine had been there all the time.

Jack thought about what she had said. She, and everyone else, knew that Mr. Potney always took a shower at about a quarter to eleven each night. Jack looked at the clock on the wall. The time was now five minutes after eleven. It was only a minute or so after

eleven when Elaine's cry had awakened him. So, whoever had stolen the vase must have done so between a quarter to eleven and eleven o'clock.

There was a mirror on the wall by the clock. Jack caught sight of his mussed hair, sticking out in all directions from when he had been asleep. He tried combing it with his fingers. Then he went back into the other room.

"Elaine," he said, "did you see anyone go upstairs while you were watching television?"

"No," she replied. "You can't see the stairs from where I was sitting."

"Did you see or hear anything at all?"

"Well, at about a quarter to eleven, Mrs. Elson looked in and said goodnight," the girl told him.

"That's right," said Mrs. Elson, nodding her head. "I had just left the kitchen and was going to my room."

"Did you go straight to your room?"

"Oh, yes," the woman assured him.

"That's true, sir," said Stokes, the butler. "I saw Mrs. Elson as she left the kitchen, and she saw me. I was just bringing the dog in from its walk. It started to rain while I was outside, and as Mrs. Elson can tell you, I was soaking wet. I went right to my room, took off my wet clothes, and went to bed."

"Your room is right under my uncle's," said Jack, thoughtfully. "Did you hear anyone walking around up there?"

"No," said Stokes. "I was already asleep when Julian and Mrs. Elson pounded at my door and said they'd heard shouts. I thought there was a fire, so I just threw on my robe and slippers and rushed out."

Jack looked at the chauffeur. "What about you, Julian? Where were you from about a quarter to eleven to eleven o'clock?"

Julian wriggled nervously. "I said goodnight to Stokes about ten-thirty. I was in my room reading, until I heard Miss Martin call out."

"I see," said Jack, slowly. He had a good idea who the thief was!

Do *you* know who it was?

How Jack solved the crime

Several things that Stokes said convinced Jack that the butler was the thief.

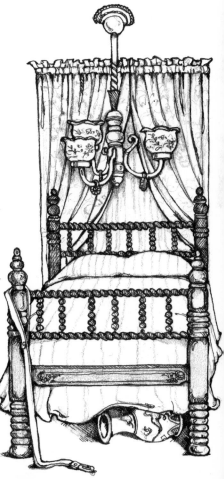

Answers

When Stokes mentioned getting soaking wet in the rain, Jack realized that the damp spots on the rug in his uncle's room, and on the stairs, could have been caused by the butler's wet shoes and dripping clothing.

Jack also realized that Stokes would have known that no one would see him if he went upstairs. Stokes knew that Julian was in his room because they had said goodnight to one another at ten-thirty. The butler also knew that Mrs. Elson would be out of the way, for he had seen her leaving for her room when he brought the dog in. And he also knew that Elaine couldn't see the stairs from where she was sitting.

So, when Stokes brought the dog in, he saw his chance. But he would have to hurry before the news show that Elaine was watching ended. He took a knife from the kitchen, hurried upstairs, and stole the vase. Then he went to his room, got out of his wet clothes and put on his pajamas. But instead of going to bed, he waited to see what would happen.

But, because he was a neat person, Stokes combed his hair. This, too, was a clue for Jack. For, when Jack looked into the mirror he saw that his hair was mussed from sleeping. Stokes had said that he had been asleep, but his hair was neatly combed. Jack knew that if Stokes had been asleep, his hair, too, would have been mussed.

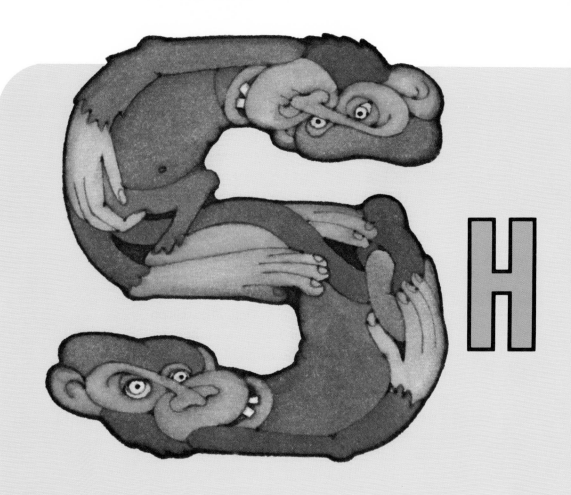

H

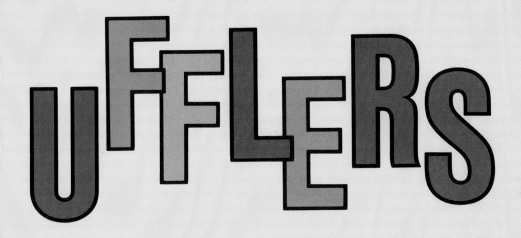

One meaning of the word "shuffle" is "to move something around, this way and that." And this is what you do to solve these puzzles. The puzzles show you how to make shapes and designs out of toothpicks, coins, or buttons. Then you have to change the shapes to something else. To make the change, you just shuffle, or move, the coins or toothpicks around until you have the right shape.

Sounds easy? Don't be too sure! Sometimes it will seem that you simply *can't* change the shape the way the puzzle wants you to! But keep trying—it can be done. And, be sure to read each puzzle carefully, for sometimes there's a clue hidden in what the puzzle says.

The spilled ice cream

Arrange two toothpicks and a large coin or button like this:

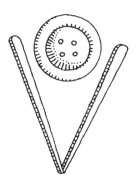

Think of this shape as an ice-cream cone with one scoop of ice cream in it. Can you move one toothpick so that the ice-cream cone is upside down and the ice cream (the coin) is no longer inside the cone?

(answer on page 134)

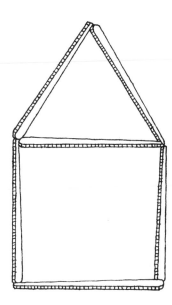

House into squares

Using six toothpicks, make a "house" like this:
Now, moving only two toothpicks, change the "house" into five squares.

(answer on page 134)

Save the sea horse!

Using nine toothpicks, make a "fish" like the one shown here:

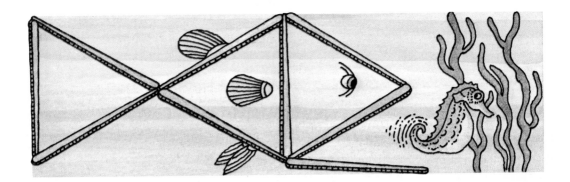

This fish is hungry! As you can see, its mouth is open and it's about to swallow a baby sea horse! Can you save the sea horse by changing the fish into four triangles, as shown below? But to do this, you may move only *three* toothpicks!

(answer on page 134)

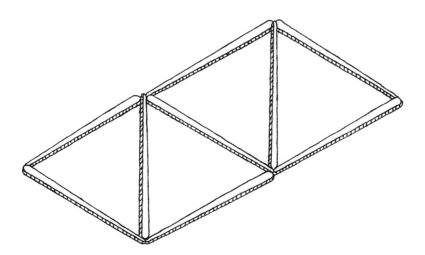

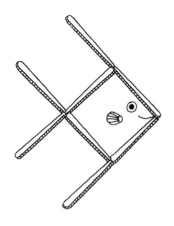

Turn the fish

Arrange eight toothpicks to make a "tropical fish," as shown at left.

When you finish, the fish will be swimming to your right. Can you turn it around, so it's swimming to your left? But to do this, you may move only *three* toothpicks!

(answer on page 134)

A toothpick creature

With thirteen toothpicks, make a toothpick creature like the one shown here.

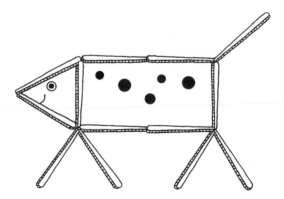

The toothpick creature is looking to your left. Can you make it look to the right, by moving only two of the toothpicks? (This is tricky!)

(answer on page 134)

The Chubbs and Slimms

With eighteen toothpicks, make two "houses" and a "yard" as shown below. Place four buttons, as shown, for "trees."

The house on the left belongs to the Chubb family. The house on the right belongs to the Slimm family. Each family owns half the yard. But they can't figure out how to divide it so that each family will have two trees. Using no more than three toothpicks, build a fence that will divide the yard into two equal parts, with two trees in each part.

(answer on page 135)

A toothpick jail

With four toothpicks, make a square, as shown above. Put three small buttons or coins inside the square, as shown.

The square is a "jail," and the buttons or coins are "prisoners." But each prisoner must be in a separate cell. Using two more toothpicks, but without letting any toothpicks cross each other, make "walls" inside the jail so that each prisoner is in a separate cell.

(answer on page 135)

Ice-cream sundae

Arrange four toothpicks and a small button or coin this way:

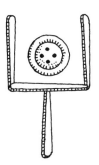

This is an ice-cream sundae glass with a cherry in it! Can you turn the glass upside down and get the cherry out by moving only two toothpicks?

(answer on page 135)

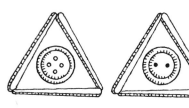

Too many monkeys

1. For this puzzle you will need nine toothpicks and four small buttons or coins. Arrange the toothpicks to make three triangles. Put a button inside each triangle. One button is left over.

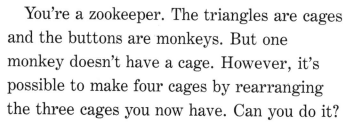

You're a zookeeper. The triangles are cages and the buttons are monkeys. But one monkey doesn't have a cage. However, it's possible to make four cages by rearranging the three cages you now have. Can you do it?

2. This puzzle is a little harder. You need twelve toothpicks and six buttons. With the toothpicks, make four triangles. Put one button in each triangle. Two are left over.

Can you rearrange the triangles so that there are six cages—one for each monkey?

(answer on page 135)

Triangle teasers

An equilateral (ee kwuh LAT uhr uhl) triangle
is a triangle that has three equal sides. It's
easy to make an equilateral triangle with
three toothpicks. You just put them together
like this:

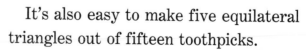

It's also easy to make five equilateral
triangles out of fifteen toothpicks.

But—

1. Can you make *five* equilateral triangles out of only *nine* toothpicks? (Here's a hint—the triangles don't all have to be the same size.)

2. Can you make *six* equilateral triangles using only *six* toothpicks? (No, you can't break any of the toothpicks in two!)

3. Can you make *eight* equilateral triangles with only *six* toothpicks? It can be done!

A triangle doesn't have to be equilateral, with all sides equal, of course. It can have two sides equal and one side different, as shown at right. This kind of triangle is called an isosceles (eye SAHS uh leez) triangle.

4. Using three toothpicks, make an isosceles triangle with two open angles at the bottom corners, like this:

Can you add two more toothpicks so as to make a total of ten triangles? Here's a hint—some triangles will be inside others.

(answers on pages 136-137)

Square stuff

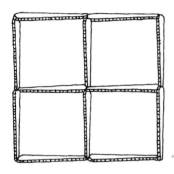

For each of the first four puzzles, arrange twelve toothpicks to make four squares, as shown at left.

1. Take away two toothpicks from the four squares, so that only two squares are left.

2. Take away four toothpicks from the four squares. Now, put them back so that there are three squares, all the same size.

3. Take away three toothpicks from the four squares. Now, put them back so there are three squares, all the same size.

4. Now, arrange the twelve toothpicks to form seven squares. (Here's a hint—all the squares won't be the same size.)

For each of the next two puzzles, arrange seventeen toothpicks to make six squares, like this:

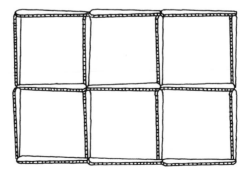

5. Take five toothpicks from the six squares, so that only three squares, all the same size, are left.

6. Take six toothpicks from the six squares so that only two squares are left.

For each of the next three puzzles, arrange twenty-four toothpicks into nine squares, like this:

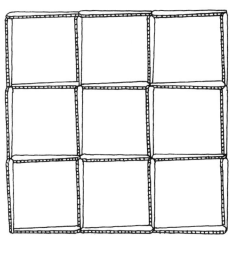

7. Take four toothpicks from the nine squares so that only five squares, all the same size, are left.

8. Take eight toothpicks from the nine squares so that only five squares, all the same size, are left.

9. Take eight toothpicks from the nine squares so that only two squares are left.

10. For this puzzle, arrange eleven toothpicks to make three squares, as shown at left. By moving three toothpicks, change the three squares into two squares.

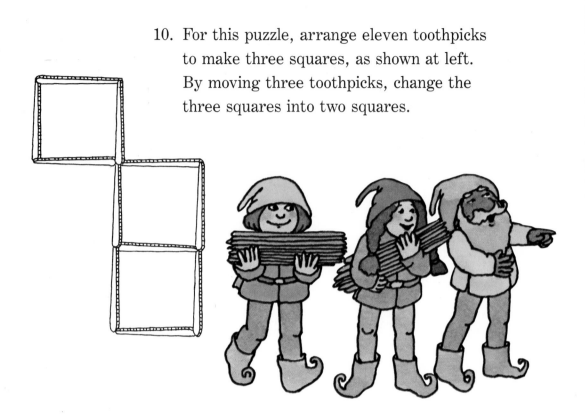

11. For this puzzle, arrange sixteen toothpicks to make five squares, like this:

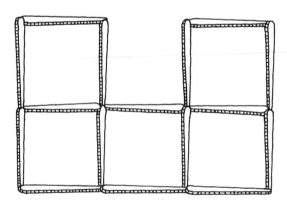

By moving three toothpicks, change the five squares into four squares, all the same size.

12. For this puzzle, arrange twenty toothpicks to make seven squares, like this:

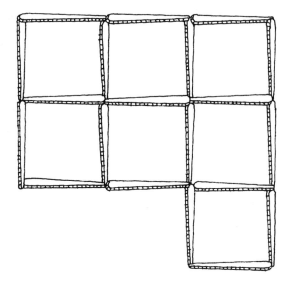

By moving three toothpicks, change the seven squares into five squares, all the same size.

(answers on pages 138-139)

Six squares

Arrange twelve toothpicks to form a large square, as shown at right. Now, can you take eight more toothpicks and make six squares inside the large square?

(answer on page 139)

Tricky tasks

These puzzles are real foolers! You must think hard about what you have to do. But, once you figure them out, you can have a lot of fun fooling your friends with them.

1. Place six toothpicks in a row, an equal distance apart, like this:

   Now, add five more toothpicks in a way that will make NINE!

2. Arrange twelve toothpicks to form three squares.

   By taking away three toothpicks, and rearranging others, it is possible to make TEN!

3. Arrange sixteen toothpicks in four squares.

   Believe it or not, by taking away two toothpicks and rearranging others, you can actually end up with NONE!

(answers on page 140)

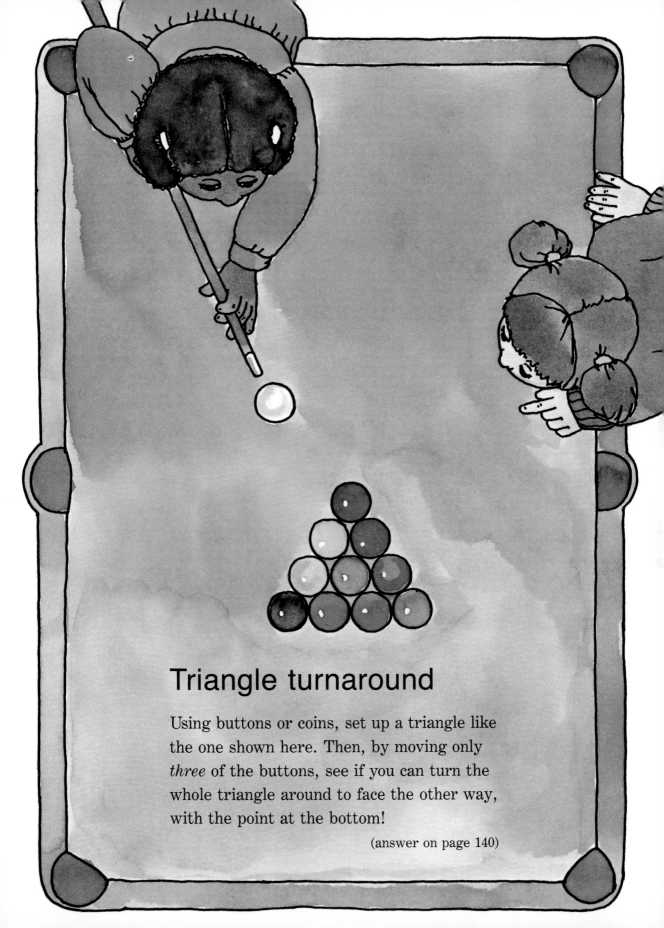

Triangle turnaround

Using buttons or coins, set up a triangle like the one shown here. Then, by moving only *three* of the buttons, see if you can turn the whole triangle around to face the other way, with the point at the bottom!

(answer on page 140)

Three in a row

1. Lay three pennies or other coins in a row. The middle coin should be tails up. The other coins should be heads up. Turning over only one coin at a time, make all three coins heads up in three moves.

2. Lay three coins in a row, as before, with the middle one tails up and the other two heads up. Turning over two coins at a time, make all the coins tails up in three moves.

3. Lay three coins in a row. Change the position of the middle coin—that is, get it out of the middle—without touching it!

(answers on page 141)

The farmer

Arrange eight toothpicks like this:

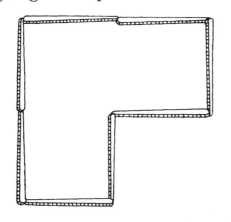

1. A prosperous farmer had a piece of land that was this shape. He wanted to divide the land into six equal parts, because he planned to grow a different crop in each part. Using five more toothpicks, can you divide the land into six equal parts?

2. One day, the farmer decided that he ought to have a will. So, he went to see his lawyer. The farmer told the lawyer that when he died, he wanted to leave one-third of his land to his wife. He wanted another third divided into two equal parts for his two sons. And he wanted to divide the last third into four equal parts for his four grandchildren.

   Using the five toothpicks you used to divide the farmer's land into six parts, can you show the lawyer how to divide the land the way the farmer wants to do it?

(answers on page 142)

One, not two

For this puzzle, you will need five toothpicks and four coins. Arrange the toothpicks in the shape of a five-pointed star, as shown at right.

Start at any toothpick. Moving clockwise, count three toothpicks. Put a coin at the end of the third toothpick.

Do this four times until four of the toothpicks have a coin. But, here's the catch—you may *never* start from a toothpick that has a coin. And you can't leave two coins at a toothpick.

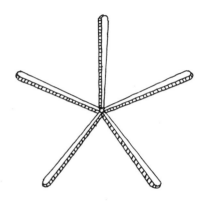

(answer on page 142)

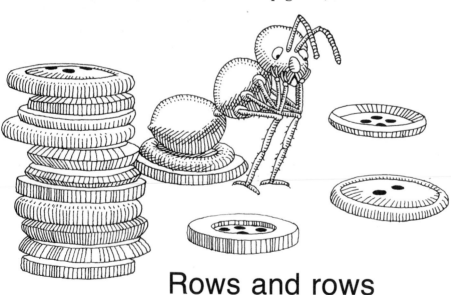

Rows and rows

Can you arrange sixteen buttons so that they form ten rows with four buttons in each row and four rows with three buttons in each row?

(answer on page 142)

Can it be done?

1. It's easy to arrange fifteen buttons in five rows with three buttons in each row.

   But can you arrange *seven* buttons in five rows with three buttons in each row?

2. It's easy to arrange twenty buttons in five rows with four buttons in each row. But can you arrange *ten* buttons in five rows with four buttons in each row?

(answers on page 143)

The mouse king's treasure

The king of the mice had a treasury. It was a big room, full of all kinds of cheese! He kept the room locked, of course. And he kept the key on a tiny island surrounded by a deep, eight-sided moat. In the moat swam deadly sharp-toothed sharks.

When the king wanted some cheese, he had his mouseketeer guards carry a small boat down to the moat. He rowed out to the island, got the key, and rowed back. When the boat wasn't in use, it was kept locked away.

The king felt sure that none of his subjects could ever get the key to the cheese treasury. But, one night, a rascally mouse by the name of Cheeky managed to steal the key! He did this using only two toothpicks.

On the opposite page, there is a picture of the moat and island. It is the same size as the king's moat and island. Using two toothpicks, see if you can figure out how Cheeky got across the moat. But remember, the toothpicks must not touch the water.

(answer on page 143)

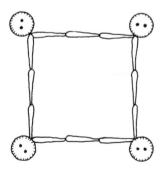

Baron Baddguy's wall

The castle of Baron Baddguy is surrounded by a square wall. At each corner of the wall there is a round tower. To make a plan of the wall and towers, arrange twelve toothpicks and four buttons, as shown at left.

Baron Baddguy wants to double the space inside the wall. But he wants the wall to be square and he wants to keep the four towers just where they are, on the outside of the wall. Can you show him how to do this?

You can use the twelve toothpicks, plus four more. You may move the toothpicks any way you wish. But the new wall must form a square and it must enclose twice as much space as the old wall. The four towers can't be moved, and must be outside the new wall.

(answer on page 143)

134

Answers

The spilled ice cream (page 110)

To turn the cone upside down, simply move one of the toothpicks to the right (or left), as shown.

House into squares (page 110)

Move the two toothpicks that form the roof so as to make a cross inside the square, as shown. This makes four small squares inside one large square, or a total of five squares.

Save the sea horse! (page 111)

The toothpicks to be moved are shown in blue.

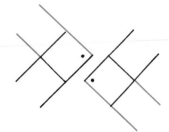

Turn the fish (page 112)

The three toothpicks that must be moved to make the fish change direction are shown in blue.

A toothpick creature (page 112)

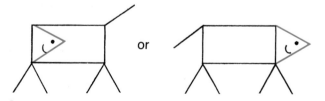

or

The Chubbs and Slimms (page 113)

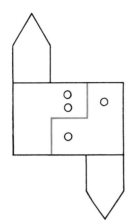

Answers

A toothpick jail (page 114)

Ice-cream sundae (page 115)

To turn the glass upside down, first slide the horizontal toothpick over, as shown in (b) below.

Then move the leftover toothpick to form the other side of the glass, as shown in (c).

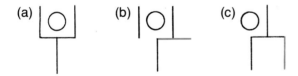

Too many monkeys (page 116)

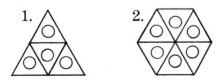

Answers

Triangle teasers (page 118)

1. To make five equilateral triangles with nine toothpicks, arrange the nine toothpicks to form four equilateral triangles, as shown below.

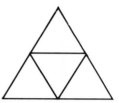

These four triangles form one large triangle, making five triangles in all.

2. To make six equilateral triangles with only six toothpicks, first make one triangle with three toothpicks, as in (a). Next, make a second triangle with the other three toothpicks, and place it point down on top of the first triangle, as shown in (b).

(a)   (b)

You now have four small equilateral triangles at each corner, plus the two large triangles, for a total of six.

3. To make eight equilateral triangles, place one three-toothpick triangle over another one, like this:

This gives you two small triangles, one at the top and one at the bottom, and four smaller ones, two on each side. That's a total of eight, counting the two you started with.

Answers

4. To make ten triangles from one isosceles triangle, add the two toothpicks as shown.

Here are the ten triangles this forms:

It is also possible to make ten triangles by placing two toothpicks this way:

Answers

Square stuff (page 120)

The toothpicks that were taken away, or moved, are shown in blue.

1.

2.

3.

4. To form seven squares with twelve toothpicks, arrange two squares of four toothpicks each, with the corners touching, as shown in (a).

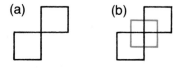

Lay a third four-toothpick square over the other two squares, as shown in (b). This forms four smaller squares, for a total of seven.

5.

6.

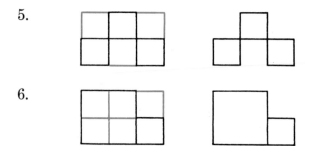

7.

8.

9.

or

10.

11.

12.

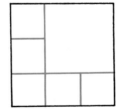

Six squares (page 123)

Answers

Tricky tasks (page 124)

1. To add five toothpicks to the six and make NINE, place the five toothpicks as shown by the blue lines.

2. Here's how to make TEN out of three squares by taking away two toothpicks and rearranging the others.

3. Here's how to make NONE out of four squares by taking away two toothpicks and rearranging the others.

Triangle turn-around (page 125)

Move the end buttons on the bottom row to the second row. Move the button that's on top to the bottom.

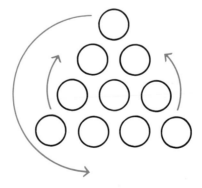

Three in a row (page 126)

1.

(a) Turn over the coin on the right.

(b) Turn over the coin in the middle.

(c) Turn over the coin on the right.

2.

(a) Turn over the coins on the ends.

(b) Turn over the coin in the middle and the
    coin on the right.

(c) Turn over the coin in the middle and the
    coin on the right.

3. Move the coin on the left (or right) so that the
   middle coin becomes an outside coin without
   being touched.

Answers

The farmer (page 127)

1. The five toothpicks that divide the shape into six parts are shown in blue.

(a) (b)

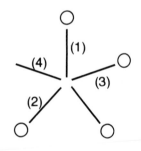

(c)

2. To divide the shape into thirds, place two toothpicks as shown in (a) at left.

Leave one-third for the farmer's wife. Using one toothpick, divide another third in half for the farmer's sons, as shown in (b).

Divide the last third into four equal parts by placing one toothpick across another as shown in (c).

One, not two (page 128)

The trick is to count in a clockwise direction. Always start with the toothpick that comes after the one by which you have just put a coin.

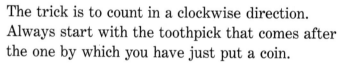

In the diagram at left, (1) shows where you might start counting for your first move. A coin is placed at the third toothpick. Continuing in a clockwise direction, count from the toothpick marked (2), and place another coin. And so on.

Rows and rows (page 128)

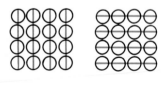

Arrange the buttons as shown at left.

There are four rows of four buttons each, running from top to bottom. There are four rows of four buttons each, running from left to right. And there are two rows of four buttons running diagonally. That's ten rows.

In addition, there are four other diagonal rows of three buttons each.

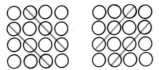

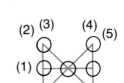

Can it be done? (page 129)

1. Arrange the seven buttons as shown at right. This gives you five rows of three buttons, as shown by the blue lines.

2. Arrange the ten buttons as shown. This gives you five rows of four buttons, as shown by the blue lines.

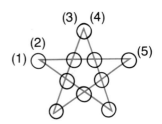

The mouse king's treasure (page 130)

First, Cheeky placed one toothpick across an angle of the pond so that ends rested on the ground. Then he placed the second toothpick with one end resting on the first toothpick and the other end resting on the island, as shown. Thus, he was able to scamper across the second toothpick, get the key, and scamper back.

Baron Baddguy's wall (page 132)

The new wall, made of sixteen toothpicks, is shown in black. The old wall is shown in blue. The new wall encloses exactly twice as much space as the old wall. The towers haven't been moved, and are still outside the wall.

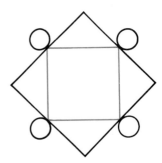

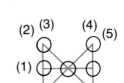

The word *ponder* means "to think over, carefully." And that's what it takes to solve these puzzles.

In some of the puzzles you have to move things from one place to another, in a certain way. There really aren't any clues in this kind of puzzle. It might help if you used buttons or other objects, to stand for the things being moved. Then you could try moving them in different ways.

In other puzzles you have to decide what

DERERS

kind of question someone might ask to get a certain answer. There aren't any clues for this kind of puzzle, either. You have to ask yourself questions and see what the answers might be. Sooner or later, you'll get an idea of what the right sort of question is.

And one or two of the puzzles are really just based on common sense. You have to ask yourself, "How would *I* do this?"

Don't give up too easily. When you solve one of these puzzles you really can be proud.

How many carnations?

Wilfred McDoodle was color blind. Red and green both looked gray to him.

Wilfred got a job working for a florist. One day, when he was all alone in the store, a lady came in and wanted to buy either two red or two green carnations. She didn't care which color they were so long as they were both the same.

Wilfred knew there were a dozen red carnations and a dozen green carnations all mixed together in the refrigerator in the back room of the store. But the red and green carnations all looked the same to him. Would he have to bring all two dozen carnations so the lady could pick out two of the same color?

What is the smallest number of carnations Wilfred would have to bring back to be sure of having two of the same color?

(answer on page 166)

The hungry rabbit

A rabbit was making a long journey across a plain. There was absolutely nothing on the plain for her to eat. By the time she was halfway across, she was starving. She was much too weak to keep going.

However, halfway across the plain there was a small house. The owner of the house was a cabbage farmer. In the yard next to the house was a big pile of cabbages. They were surrounded by a square fence.

The rabbit had to eat or she would soon die. She was thin enough to squeeze through the fence and get to the cabbages. But if she went into the enclosure and ate as much as she needed, she would be too fat to get back out. The farmer would probably kill her. And the cabbages were all too big to be pushed through the fence to the outside.

What can the rabbit do?

(answer on page 166)

The people of Tuffleheim

Long ago, a traveler walking along a road met a man coming the other way. "Hello, friend," called the man. "Where are you heading?"

"I'm going to the town of Tuffleheim," said the traveler.

"Oh, you'll need to be careful, there," warned the other man. "That town has been enchanted by a wicked magician! Half the people can tell only the truth, and the other half can tell only lies. You never know whom to believe in Tuffleheim."

"I'll be careful," said the traveler.

An hour later, he reached Tuffleheim. It was getting late, and he was tired and hungry. He wanted to find a good inn where he could have a nice dinner and a comfortable room in which to spend the night. In any other town, he would have simply asked someone for the name of the best inn. But he couldn't do that, here. For, if the person he asked should happen to be one of the liars, he would send the traveler to the *worst* inn.

The traveler realized he would have to first find out whether anyone he talked to was a liar or a truth-teller. He went up to the first Tuffleheimer he saw and asked her a question. What question could the traveler have asked that would let him know, at once, whether a person was a liar or a truth-teller?

(answer on page 167)

The outlaws
and the marshals

Sheriff Dalton of Dry Gulch heard that two U.S. marshals were searching for some outlaws near his town. He decided to ride out and see if he could help them.

After a time, he saw a campfire with four men around it. Riding closer, he saw that two of the men were tied up and two were untied.

"Are you the marshals?" he called to the untied men.

One of the men said something, but Sheriff

Dalton couldn't hear him. "What did you say?" he called.

The second man answered. "He said that we're the marshals."

Suddenly, one of the tied-up men began to struggle. "That's not true!" he yelled. "*We're* the marshals! We set out to capture these two, but they ambushed us! They're the outlaws!"

Sheriff Dalton knew that the marshals would always tell the truth. He also knew that the outlaws would always tell lies. How could he know from what the men said, which ones were really the marshals and which ones were the outlaws?

(answer on page 167)

The Kiki and the Google

Captain Laura Blazer, the Space Ranger, was in trouble. She was lost on the planet Raz. Her scout ship had run out of power and come down on an unknown part of the planet.

Captain Blazer could call her base by radio. If she could let the base know where she was, another ship could be sent to rescue her. But she knew only that she was in the forest where the creatures known as Kikis and Googles lived.

Not much was known about these creatures. They were intelligent, and could talk. But, for some reason, they never answered more than one question from a stranger. It was also known that while Kikis always told the truth, Googles always lied.

Captain Blazer had never seen either a Kiki
or a Google. But she knew they did not look
alike. And she knew that the land of the Kikis
was in one part of the forest and the land of
the Googles in another part. If she could find
out which country she was in, she could let
her base know where she was.

She began to walk through the strange
forest. Suddenly, she came face to face with
two odd looking creatures. One must be a Kiki
and the other a Google. But which was which?

Because she was a stranger, they would
answer only one question. One of them would
lie and the other would tell the truth. What
one question could Captain Blazer ask that
would let her know whether she was in the
land of the Kikis or the land of the Googles?

(answer on page 167)

Sooba the cider seller

Cider is the national drink of the land of Bulgravia. On the main street of every town there's at least one cider shop. The cider is kept in big barrels. It's sold in amounts known as "guzzles." (A guzzle is about equal to one cup or 250 milliliters, but that isn't important.)

One day, a customer came into the cider shop of a lady named Sooba. The customer had a large bucket. He asked Sooba to put exactly four guzzles of cider into the bucket.

Sooba took the bucket to the cider barrel. Next to the barrel there was a three-guzzle pitcher and a five-guzzle pitcher. How could Sooba measure out exactly four guzzles of cider?

(answer on page 168)

The clever old woman

Long ago, in the days when people used candles to light their houses, there lived an old woman. She was poor, but very clever. She thought of many ways to save money.

One way she saved money was by making new candles from old ones. She found that one-fourth of a candle never burned because it was inside the candleholder. Most people just threw away these unburned candle stubs. But the old woman saved hers. By melting four of these stubs, she could make one new candle!

One day, the old woman went to the candlemaker's shop and bought sixteen candles. How many new candles could she make from the left-over fourths of the sixteen candles?

(answer on page 168)

Caspuccio the bandit

In the kingdom of Cappedonia, there was a daring bandit named Caspuccio. But he robbed only barons, earls, and wealthy nobles. And he gave much of the money he stole to poor people who needed it. So, most common people liked him. Of course, the barons and earls hated him.

Finally, Caspuccio was captured. He was taken before King Bombaso, for trial. All the barons and earls came to the trial. So did many common people.

"So, this is the famous robber, Caspuccio," said the king. "What shall we do with him?"

"Hang him!" yelled all the barons.

"Cut off his head!" shouted the earls.

"Set him free!" cried the common people.

"Well, I must be fair about this," said the king. "I'll give everyone a chance to have their way. Caspuccio, I want you to make a statement. In other words, *tell* me something. If what you say is true, you'll be hanged, as the barons want. If what you say is false, you'll have your head cut off, as the earls want. But if I can't decide if it's true or false, you'll go free, as the common people want."

Caspuccio knew he didn't have much of a chance. After all, every statement is either true or false! The king could say that what Caspuccio said was either true or false.

Caspuccio thought for a few moments. Then, a smile came over his face. He spoke seven words. And after thinking about what he said for a while, the king set him free!

What did Caspuccio say?

(answer on page 168)

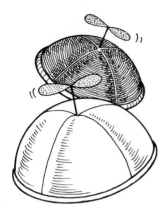

The magical beanies

There are two girls, named Kim and Hannah, and three boys, named Mark, Frank, and John. They are all wearing beanie caps. Some of the caps are red and some are white. Each child can see only the other children's caps.

The beanies are magical. Anyone wearing a white beanie can tell only the truth. Anyone wearing a red beanie can tell only a lie.

Frank says, "I see three red beanies and two white ones."

Mark says, "I see four white beanies."

Hannah says, "I see three red beanies and one white one."

Kim says, "I see one red and three whites."

John says, "I see what Hannah sees."

From what the children said, can you tell the color of the beanie each one was wearing?

(answer on page 169)

The three musicians

Long ago, in China, three musicians were traveling to the city of Peking. They had been hired to perform at a wedding there.

The three came to a wide river. They were shocked to see that the bridge had collapsed. There was no way to get across the river. The musicians knew that the nearest bridge was far down the river, nearly a day's walk away. But they had to be in Peking in a few hours.

Suddenly, they saw two children rowing a boat down the river. The musicians called to the children, offering to pay them to use the boat. The children rowed to the shore.

However, the boat was *very* small. It could hold only two children or one grown-up. This was a serious problem. If one of the musicians took the boat across the river, there would be no way to send the boat back. A grown-up couldn't take a child and then send the child back with the boat—for a grown-up and child couldn't both get into the boat at the same time.

But one of the children had an idea. And in less than an hour, all three musicians were across the river. How did they do it?

(answer on page 170)

Abdul's journeys

An Arab named Abdul made a journey from his home to another part of the desert.

For the first half of the journey, Abdul got to ride in a truck. It was a one-hour ride. And going by truck was ten times faster than Abdul could have walked the same distance.

However, for the second half of the journey, Abdul had to ride an old, lame camel. That part of the trip took him twice as long as if he had walked.

When Abdul went back home, he had to walk all the way. Which of the two trips was quickest? How much time did each trip take?

(answer on page 170)

The bad bears

One day, Mrs. Bear went to market and left her four little cubs, Bruno, Boffin, Bobo, and Bilda, alone in the house. Of course, the four got into mischief! When Mrs. Bear returned, she found a broken honeypot and a big puddle of honey on the living room floor!

"Who broke the honeypot?" demanded Mrs. Bear.

"I didn't do it," cried Bruno.

"Bobo did it," claimed Boffin.

"Bilda did it," said Bobo.

"Bobo's lying!" exclaimed Bilda.

Three of the little bears are lying. One is telling the truth. Who is telling the truth? And which bear broke the honeypot?

(answer on page 171)

The brave clown

The guard at the bridge looked surprised.
Then he smiled. Walking down the road came
a chubby clown, juggling three colored balls!

Then the guard stopped smiling. He saw
that the clown intended to cross the bridge.

"Wait!" he said. "How much do you weigh?"

"Why, exactly 198 pounds (89.10 kilograms)
with my costume on," answered the clown.

The guard felt one of the colored balls.
"This weighs at least a pound (0.45 kg)," he
said. "So you and the balls together weigh 201
pounds (90.45 kg)." He shook his head. "I'm
sorry, but you can't cross the bridge."

"Why not?" asked the clown in wonder.

"Because the bridge will hold only 200
pounds (90 kg)," said the guard. "Any more
than that and it will collapse. You would fall to
your death in the deep canyon! That's why I'm
here—to make sure that no one who's too
heavy tries to cross the bridge."

"I've got to cross," said the clown. "My
circus act starts in a few minutes! I must
hurry!"

"Leave the balls behind."

The clown shook his head. "I can't. I need
them for my act."

Suddenly, the clown smiled. "I know how I
can do it," he exclaimed.

How did the clown cross the bridge safely?

(answer on page 171)

The Ping-Pong and the Biggie

Explorers from earth landed on a far-off planet. They were amazed to find that all the creatures on the planet were shaped like balls! These creatures couldn't bounce, but they could move by rolling.

The smartest creatures were about the size of a ping-pong ball. The earth people called them "Ping-Pongs." There was another kind of creature that was ten times bigger than a Ping-Pong. The earth people called these things "Biggies." They noticed that anytime a Biggie saw a Ping-Pong, the Biggie would try to roll over the little Ping-Pong and crush it!

The earth people built a small, one-room hut to live in while they were on the planet. When they left the planet, they left this hut empty, with the door open.

One day, a Ping-Pong came rolling into the hut. It was amazed by the square room with the four sharp corners. Ping-Pongs had never imagined such a thing.

Suddenly, a Biggie came rolling into the hut. It was between the Ping-Pong and the door—the only way out. The Ping-Pong was trapped! The Biggie rolled toward it!

But the Ping-Pong was clever. It found a way to keep the Biggie from rolling over it. What did the Ping-Pong do?

(answer on page 171)

Answers

How many carnations? (page 146)

The smallest number of carnations Wilfred McDoodle would have to bring back would be *three*. When he picked out two carnations, they might both be the same color, but one might be red and one might be green. Therefore, by taking along a third flower that would be either red or green, he would be sure of having two carnations of the same color.

The hungry rabbit (page 147)

The rabbit must squeeze through the fence. She must push as many cabbages as she needs up to the fence. Then she can go back outside and eat the cabbages through the fence.

The people of Tuffleheim (page 149)

The traveler must ask a question to which he knows the answer. Then he will know whether the answer he got was true or false. He could ask a question with an obvious answer, such as "Is it daytime?" or "Am I a man?" A truth-teller would, of course, give the right answer, but a liar would reveal himself by giving an answer the traveler knows is wrong.

The outlaws and the marshals (page 150)

The sheriff knew that if the man who answered first had been an outlaw, he would have lied and said that he was a marshal. And if he were a marshal, he would have told the truth. So, whichever way, he would have said that he and the other untied man were marshals.

Therefore, when the other untied man told the sheriff that the first man had said they were marshals, he was obviously telling the truth. But if he had been an outlaw, he would have lied. Thus, the sheriff knew the two untied men were indeed the marshals and the other two men were the outlaws.

The Kiki and the Google (page 152)

The question Captain Blazer asked was, "Is this your country?" If she were in the land of the truthful Kikis, both creatures would answer "Yes." The Kiki would be telling the truth and the Google would be lying. If she were in the land of the lying Googles, both creatures would answer "No." Again, the Kiki would be telling the truth and the Google would be lying. In either case, Captain Blazer would know where she was.

Answers

Sooba the cider seller (page 154)

Sooba filled the three-guzzle pitcher and poured the three guzzles into the bucket. Then she filled the three-guzzle pitcher again and poured the three guzzles into the five-guzzle pitcher. She filled the three-guzzle pitcher a third time. She then poured the cider into the five-guzzle pitcher until it was filled. It took two guzzles to fill the five-guzzle pitcher (with the three already in it), which left exactly one guzzle in the three-guzzle pitcher. Sooba poured the one guzzle into the bucket, which already had three guzzles in it. She now had four guzzles in the bucket.

The clever old woman (page 155)

The clever old woman made five new candles. Every four candles gave her four-fourths from which to make one new candle. So, from the sixteen candles she made four new ones. But, those four candles also gave her four-fourths from which she made a fifth candle.

Caspuccio the bandit (page 156)

Caspuccio said, "You're going to cut off my head."

If the King said this was true, he'd have to behead Caspuccio to *make* it true. But he had said that the bandit would be hanged for making a true statement. However, if Caspuccio were hanged, that would make his statement false—which would mean he should have been beheaded, making the statement true after all! So, the king couldn't decide whether the statement was true or false. He had to let Caspuccio go!

Answers

The magical beanies (page 158)

Frank said he could see three red beanies and two white ones. But that's *five* beanies. And Frank can see only the beanies on the four other children, not his own. So he's lying, which means that he's wearing a red beanie.

Mark says he can see four white beanies. But we know that Frank is wearing a red beanie. Mark is lying when he says he sees only white beanies. So, Mark is also wearing a red beanie.

Kim says she sees one red and three white beanies. But both Frank and Mark have red ones. Kim is lying when she says she sees only one red beanie, so we know she's wearing a red beanie.

We know Frank, Mark, and Kim are wearing red beanies, so Hannah is telling the truth when she says she sees three red beanies. And we know that at least two of the children are wearing white beanies, so Hannah must be telling the truth when she says she sees one—otherwise, she would be wearing a red beanie and would have to lie about the white one.

John must be wearing the one white beanie Hannah sees, so he's a truth-teller, too. Thus, when he says he sees the same thing Hannah does, we know for sure that she has a white beanie on.

Frank, Mark, and Kim are wearing red beanies. Hannah and John are wearing white beanies.

Answers

The three musicians (page 158)

First, the two children rowed to the other side of the river. One of them got out of the boat, and the other rowed back.

The first musician then rowed the boat across. When he reached the other side, the child who was there got into the boat and rowed it back.

Next, the two children took the boat across the river again. Again, one of them stayed there while the other brought the boat back. The second musician then rowed across.

This was done one more time, until all three musicians and one child were across the river. The musicians paid the child, who then rowed back across the river to his friend.

Abdul's journeys (page 160)

It was actually quicker for Abdul to walk than it was for him to go by truck and camel!

For the first journey, going half the distance by truck took one hour. This was ten times faster than Abdul could have walked. In other words, Abdul could have walked halfway in ten hours. Therefore, if his camel ride was twice as slow as walking, it must have taken twenty hours. So altogether, Abdul's first journey took twenty-one hours.

If Abdul could walk halfway in ten hours, it obviously took him twenty hours to walk the whole way. So his homeward journey, walking, took only twenty hours—one hour less than his first journey.

The bad bears (page 161)

If Bruno is telling the truth when he says that he didn't break the pot, then the other three statements are false. This means that Bobo is lying when he says Bilda broke the pot. However, this makes Bilda's statement, that Bobo is lying, true. We know that three of the bears are lying, so there can't be two true statements.

Therefore, Bruno's statement must be false, which means he broke the honeypot. Thus, Boffin's claim that Bobo broke it is false. So is Bobo's claim that Bilda broke it. Bilda's statement that Bobo is lying is the true one.

Answers

The brave clown (page 162)

The clown juggled the balls as he walked across the bridge. This way, one of the balls was always in the air. Thus, the weight of the clown and the other two balls was exactly 200 pounds (90.45 kg), which the bridge could hold.

The Ping-Pong and the Biggie (page 164)

The Ping-Pong rolled into a corner. Because the Biggie was ten times bigger than the Ping-Pong, it could not fit into as small an angle as the Ping-Pong, as shown below. The Ping-Pong stayed in the corner until the Biggie grew tired and left.

TWISTERS

The puzzles you are about to do are brain *twisters!* It may seem as if some of them are *impossible* to solve—but all of them can be solved. There are lots of clues, but you have to sort out all the clues. You have to think about what each clue really means. And you may have to fit them together in different ways to find the answer.

It is best to use pencil and paper, so that you can write all the clues down and keep them straight in your mind. In some cases, it will be a big help if you draw diagrams or pictures. In some cases, you can solve the puzzle by just crossing out clues, until the right answer suddenly pops out at you!

A crowd of cows

If you were to see a cow in front of two cows, a cow behind two cows, and a cow between two cows, how many cows would you see altogether?

(answer on page 187)

Chipper's relative

A raccoon named Chatter saw a friend of his, named Chipper, talking to a young raccoon. As Chatter neared them, the young raccoon trotted off.

"Who was that little raccoon you were just talking to?" asked Chatter.

"Why, that raccoon's father is my father's only son," answered Chipper.

In what way were Chipper and the young raccoon related to one another?

(answer on page 187)

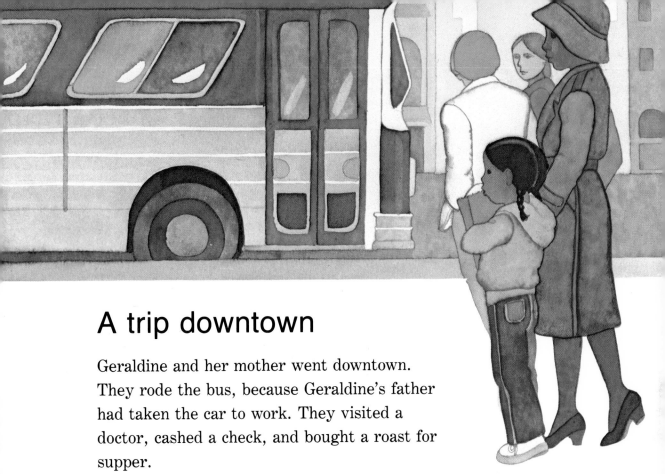

A trip downtown

Geraldine and her mother went downtown. They rode the bus, because Geraldine's father had taken the car to work. They visited a doctor, cashed a check, and bought a roast for supper.

Geraldine's father doesn't work on Saturday or Sunday. The doctor's office is closed on Wednesday. The bank where the check was cashed is open Monday, Wednesday, Friday, and Saturday. The butcher shop is closed on Friday. What day did Geraldine and her mother go downtown?

(answer on page 187)

Ginny and Sarah

Sarah is now the same age that Ginny was four years ago. Four years ago, Ginny was twice as old as Sarah. Ginny is now twelve. How old is Sarah?

(answer on page 187)

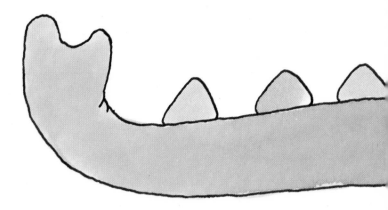

The creatures of Zorp

On the planet Zorp, far off in another part of space, there are four kinds of creatures. Each kind of creature has a different number of legs.

- Whoofers have two more legs than Sizzles.

- Zompers have two more legs than Whoofers.

- Sizzles have two more legs than Yeeples.

- Yeeples have six fewer legs than Zompers.

How many legs does each kind of Zorpian creature have?

(answer on page 188)

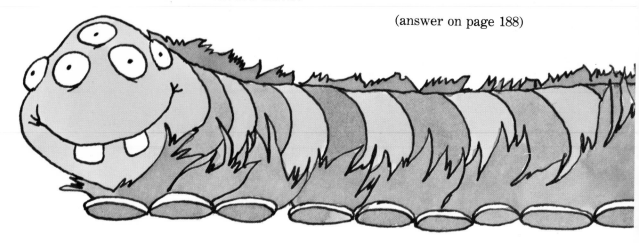

Black and white kittens

Marilyn's cat has had a litter of kittens. Some are all black and some are all white. Each black kitten has the same number of white brothers and sisters as black ones. But each white kitten has twice as many black brothers and sisters as white ones. How many kittens are in the litter?

(answer on page 188)

The new kids

A new family had moved into the neighborhood. When Mrs. Frisby, a neighbor, passed the house, she saw four children playing in the yard. She could tell they were brothers and sisters, for they all looked very much alike.

"My, what a nice, big family," she exclaimed. "What are your names and ages?"

"I'm Carl," said a boy. He pointed at a girl who stood beside him. "This is Jennifer. I'm a year older than she is."

"I'm George," said another boy. "I'm a year younger than my sister Susie."

"I'll be eight next month," announced Jennifer. "I'm three years younger than Susie."

How old was each child?

(answer on page 189)

A hungry bookworm

Two large books are side by side on a shelf.
The first book, on the left, contains two
hundred pages. The second book contains one
hundred pages.

A hungry bookworm got into the first book.
It ate its way through the first page of the
first book and all the way through the last
page of the second book. How many pages
(not counting the covers) did the bookworm
eat through?

(answer on page 189)

Three puppies

Three puppies were walking one behind the other. The puppies' names were Spot, Ginger, and Bingo. Spot was behind Bingo. Ginger was in front of Spot. Bingo was in front of Ginger. Which puppy was first in line?

(answer on page 189)

The great mouse race

Wheep, Squee, Eeper, Tweep, and Pweet are mice. Like all mice, they are fast runners. One day, the five mice decided to hold a race to see who was the fastest. When the race was over, here's how they finished:

- Wheep wasn't first.

- Pweet finished right behind Wheep.

- Squee wasn't second.

- Eeper came in two places after Squee.

- Tweep wasn't first or last.

Can you figure out the order in which the mice finished the race?

(answer on page 190)

Swifty and Junior

To do this puzzle, you have to know some things about animals—such as, which animals have tails and which don't, and what kinds of animals are related to each other. For example, a dog is closely related to a wolf, but it isn't very closely related to a bear.

Seven of the animals in a zoo are: a tiger, a chimpanzee, a lioness and her cub, a leopard, and a spider monkey and her baby. One of the animals is named Swifty and one is named Junior.

1. Swifty has a long tail.

2. The tiger is closely related to both Swifty and Junior.

3. Swifty has never touched Junior.

What kind of animal is Swifty?

(answer on page 190)

Shakes all around

Six children were nominated for the position of president of their school class. Doris won the election. She shook hands with each of the other children. Then, all the children shook hands with each other. How many handshakes were there altogether?

(answer on page 191)

Mr. Short, Mr. Tall, and Mr. Middle

Three friends, all men, were traveling on an airplane. They struck up a conversation with a lady who was seated near them.

"Believe it or not," said the tall man, "our last names are Tall, Short, and Middle!"

"That's right," chuckled Mr. Short. "And, as you can see, one of us is tall, one is short, and one is middle-sized. But not one of us looks like our name."

Can you figure out the name of the short man, the tall man, and the middle-sized man?

(answer on page 191)

A crowd of cows (page 174)

You would see three cows standing in a line. One would be in front of the other two, one would be behind the other two, and one would be in the middle.

Chipper's relative (page 174)

The young raccoon's father is Chipper's father's only son. If Chipper's father has only one son, that son has to be Chipper. Therefore, Chipper must be the young raccoon's father.

A trip downtown (page 175)

Geraldine's father does not work on Saturday or Sunday. We know he was at work on this day, so Saturday and Sunday are ruled out. The doctor's office is closed on Wednesday, so Wednesday is out. The bank where Geraldine's mother cashed a check is closed on Tuesday and Thursday, so these days are out. The butcher shop is closed on Friday, but Geraldine's mother bought a roast there. So, Friday is ruled out. This leaves only Monday.

Ginny and Sarah (page 175)

Ginny is now twelve. Four years ago, she was eight. If Sarah is now the same age Ginny was four years ago, Sarah is now eight.

Answers

Answers

The creatures of Zorp (page 176)

The last clue tells us that Yeeples have six fewer legs than Zompers. So, we know a Zomper has at least six legs. The second clue tells us Zompers have two more legs than Whoofers, so Whoofers must have at least four legs. And the first clue told us Whoofers have two legs more than Sizzles, so Sizzles must have at least two legs.

However, clue three said that Sizzles have two more legs than Yeeples, meaning a Yeeple must have at least two legs. Therefore, to give a Sizzle two more legs than a Yeeple, we have to give it four legs. Then, we must add two legs to each of the other two creatures. That gives us:

- Zompers: 8 legs—two more than a Whoofer.
- Whoofers: 6 legs—two more than a Sizzle.
- Sizzles: 4 legs—two more than a Yeeple.
- Yeeples: 2 legs—six less than a Zomper.

Black and white kittens (page 179)

There are seven kittens in the litter—four black and three white. Each black kitten has three black and three white brothers and sisters. Each white kitten has two white and four black brothers and sisters.

The new kids (page 179)

Jennifer announced that she would be eight next month, which means she is *now* seven. So, if she's three years younger than Susie, Susie is ten. Carl said he was a year older than Jennifer, so he is eight. And George, who is a year younger than Susie, must be nine.

A hungry bookworm (page 180)

When two books are side by side on a shelf, the *front* cover of the first book, the book on the left, is pressed against the *back* cover of the second book. A book's first page is next to its front cover and its last page is next to its back cover. So, if the bookworm ate through the first page of the first book, it then ate its way through the book's front cover. Next, it ate its way through the back cover of the second book. Then it ate through the last page of the second book. So, altogether, it ate its way through only *two* pages.

Three puppies (page 181)

The last two clues tell you that Ginger was in front of Spot and Bingo was in front of Ginger. So, Bingo was first, followed by Ginger, then Spot.

Answers

The great mouse race (page 183)

We know that Wheep wasn't first. Pweet finished right behind Wheep, so she couldn't have been first, either. Eeper came in two places after Squee, so obviously he wasn't first. And Tweep was neither first nor last. That leaves only Squee. Squee was the winner.

If Squee was first, and we know that Eeper came in two places after her, then Eeper must have come in third.

We know that Pweet finished right behind Wheep. If Wheep had finished second, that would mean that Pweet had finished third. But from what we have worked out, we know that Eeper was third. So, Wheep couldn't have come in second. He had to have come in fourth. And, if Pweet was behind him, she must have been fifth. Tweep, then, had to have been second.

So, the order of finish in the Great Mouse Race was:

1. Squee
2. Tweep
3. Eeper
4. Wheep
5. Pweet

Swifty and Junior (page 184)

Clue 1 says that Swifty has a long tail. That rules out the chimpanzee, for chimpanzees do not have a tail.

Clue 2 says the tiger is closely related to both Swifty and Junior. So, the tiger can't be Swifty or Junior. This clue also rules out the spider monkey and her baby. Tigers, lions, and leopards are close relatives. They are all cats. But monkeys and apes are primates—a very different kind of animal. So, we know that Swifty is either the lioness, her cub, or the leopard.

Clue 3 tells us that Swifty has never touched Junior. We know that the lioness and her cub must touch one another often, so neither of them can be Swifty. That leaves only the leopard.

Answers

Shakes all around (page 186)

Each handshake counts as one, even though two people are shaking hands. So, when Doris shook hands with the other five children, that was five handshakes.

Then, child number two had his hand shaken by numbers 3, 4, 5, and 6, which is four more handshakes. Child 3, in addition to shaking hands with number 2 (which has already been counted), shook hands with 4, 5, and 6, for three more handshakes. Number 4, in addition to shaking hands with 2 and 3, shook hands with 5 and 6, which is two more shakes. Numbers 5 and 6 had shaken hands will all the others, so when they shook hands with each other, that counts as the last shake.

That makes a total of fifteen handshakes.

Mr. Short, Mr. Tall, and Mr. Middle (page 186)

Both the tall man and Mr. Short spoke to the lady. So, the tall man was not Mr. Short. And because his name doesn't match his appearance, he can't be Mr. Tall. So, he must be Mr. Middle.

If Mr. Middle is the tall man, Mr. Short can't be tall. And, of course, he can't be short. So, he has to be the middle-sized man. The name of the short man, then, has to be Mr. Tall.

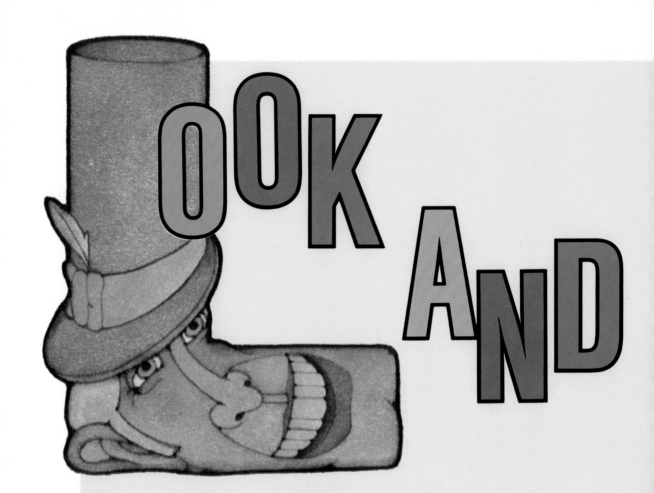

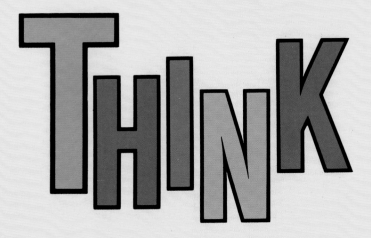

The next few puzzles have shapes for you to look at and think about. You're asked to figure out things. How would a certain shape look if it were turned around? Or, how many shapes are there inside another shape?

There are no clues for puzzles of this kind. They're much like jigsaw puzzles without pieces. To solve them, you have to be able to see in your mind how things fit together, and how shapes can be put together to make other shapes. Many people find this sort of thing very difficult. For some people, it's easy and lots of fun. Let's see how it is for you.

Seeing squares

How many squares do you see?

(answer on page 202)

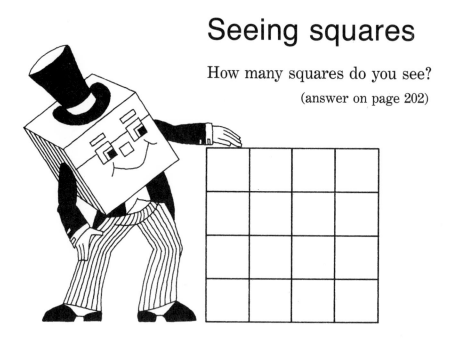

Seeing triangles

This square has been divided into triangles.
How many triangles can you find?

(answer on page 202)

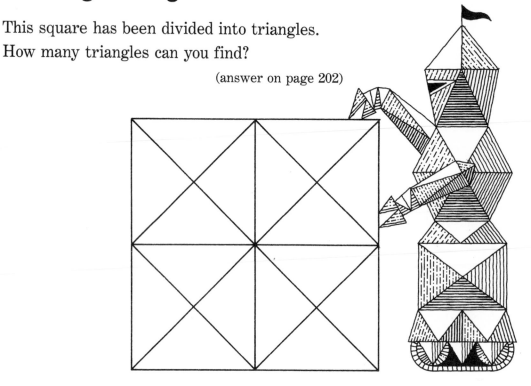

A mechanically minded squirrel

If you can figure out which way each gear is moving, you can tell whether the squirrel is pulling the basket of nuts *up* or letting it *down*. The first gear is turning in the direction of the dotted arrow. Here's a hint to get you started: the second gear will turn in the opposite direction.

(answer on page 203)

Hidden Sides

1. No matter how you look at a cube, such as
   a building block, you can see only three
   sides of it. How many sides (including top
   and bottom) does a cube have altogether?

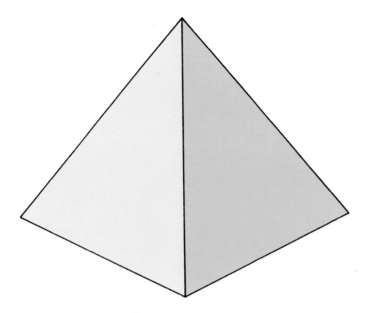

2. How many sides, including the bottom, does this pyramid have? Here's a hint—the back of the pyramid looks just like the front.

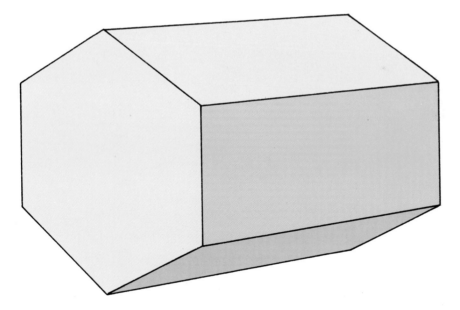

3. How many sides, including top and bottom, does this shape have? The back looks just like the front.

(answers on page 203)

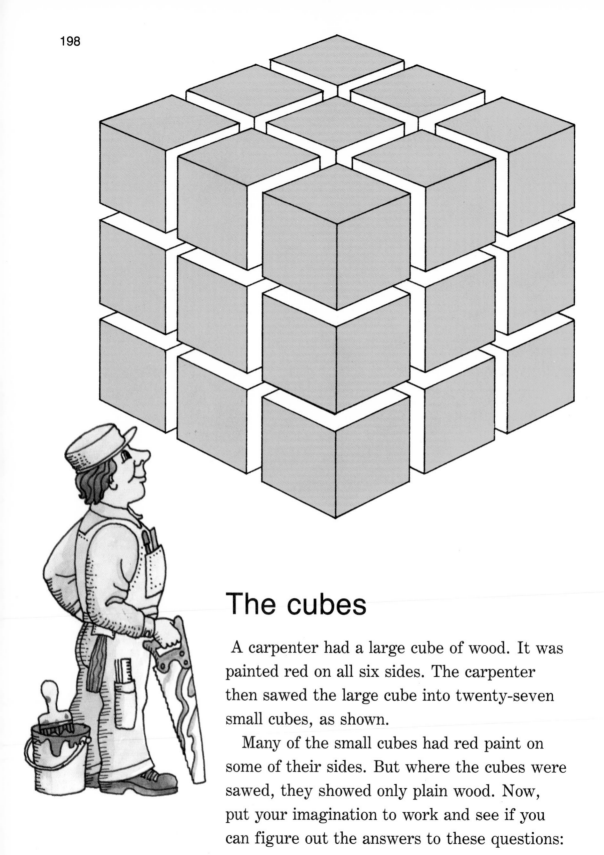

The cubes

A carpenter had a large cube of wood. It was painted red on all six sides. The carpenter then sawed the large cube into twenty-seven small cubes, as shown.

Many of the small cubes had red paint on some of their sides. But where the cubes were sawed, they showed only plain wood. Now, put your imagination to work and see if you can figure out the answers to these questions:

1. How many of the small cubes had red paint on three sides?

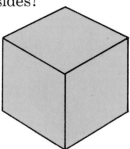

2. How many of the small cubes had red paint on two sides?

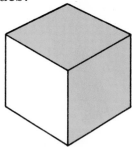

3. How many of the small cubes had red paint on only one side?

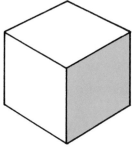

4. Were there any of the small cubes that had no paint on them at all?

(answers on page 203)

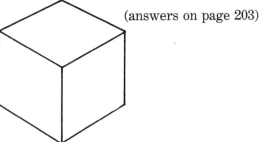

Kliggs, klaggs, and kluggs

1. Let's call this shape a "kligg." This is one side of a kligg:

Now try to turn the kligg around in your mind. Which one of the drawings below shows the other side of a kligg?

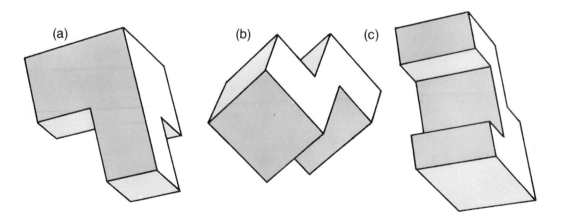

(a) (b) (c)

2. Let's call this shape
a "klagg." This is
one side of a klagg:

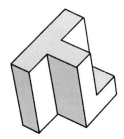

Now try to turn the klagg around in your mind. Which one of the drawings below shows the other side of a klagg?

(a) 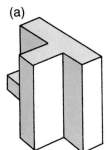   (b) 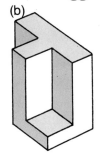   (c)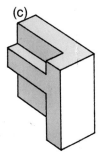

3. Let's call this shape
a "klugg." This is
one side of a klugg:

Now try to turn the klugg around in your mind. Which one of the drawings below shows the other side of a klugg?

(answers on page 203)

(a) 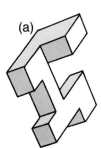   (b) 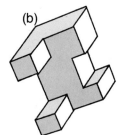   (c)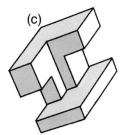

Seeing squares (page 194)

There is one large square with sixteen small squares inside it, making seventeen. But . . .

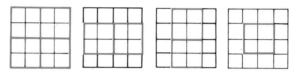

the small squares can be combined like this to make nine more squares, or a total of twenty-six squares. And . . .

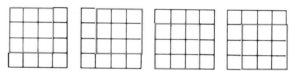

the small squares can be combined in other ways to form four slightly larger squares. So, altogether, there are thirty squares.

Seeing triangles (page 194)

There are forty-four triangles in all, as shown below.

A mechanically minded squirrel (page 195)

The arrows show the direction in which each gear is moving. The last gear is moving counterclockwise—turning toward its left—so it is pulling the basket up.

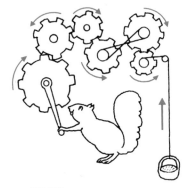

Hidden sides (page 196)

1. A cube has six sides, including the top and bottom.
2. A pyramid has five sides, including the bottom.
3. This shape has eight sides, including the top and bottom.

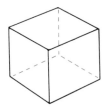
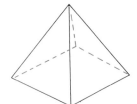
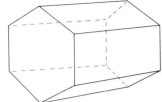

The cubes (page 198)

1. Eight cubes have red paint on three sides.
2. Twelve cubes have red paint on two sides.
3. Six cubes have red paint on one side.
4. Only one cube has no paint on it at all.

Kliggs, klaggs, and kluggs (page 200)

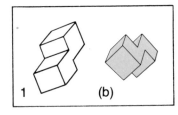
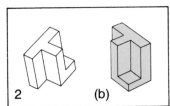
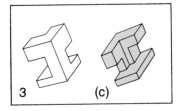

1   (b)   2   (b)   3   (c)

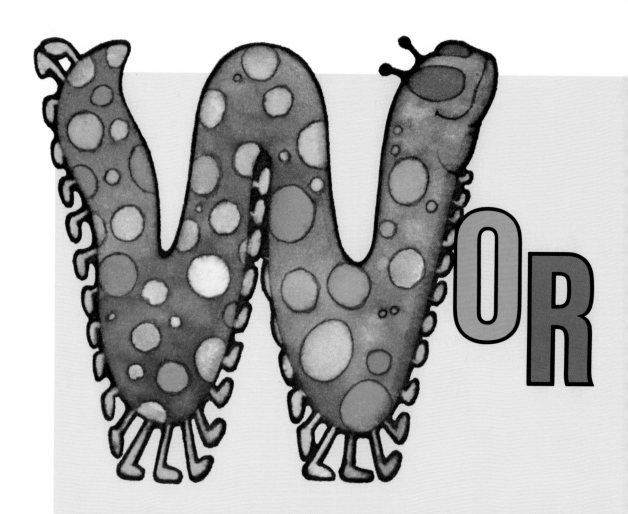
Or

As you've probably guessed, these puzzles are *word* puzzles. They ask you to find hidden words, take words apart and rearrange them, solve codes, and so on. You'll need a pencil and paper so that you can write things down.

To solve these puzzles, it helps if you know lots of words and their meanings. If you do a lot of reading, these puzzles should be fairly easy—and lots of fun.

Turnaround words

When you spell most words backwards, you get a word that doesn't mean anything, such as girl—lrig. But sometimes when you turn a word around you get a new, real word. For example, spell *rat* backwards and you get *tar*.

Here are clues to some words that become new words when they're turned around. See how many you can get.

1. Turn around a word for a number and get a word for something with which you catch fish.

2. Turn around a word for a tool to cook with and get a word for something a baby often does.

3. Turn around a word that means "at this very moment" and get a word for something that is gained by a victory.

4. Turn around the word for a thing you do work with and get the word for something pirates were always seeking.

5. Turn around a word that means "not dead," and get a word that means "very, very bad."

6. Turn around a word for someone who isn't truthful and you'll get a word for something a train needs.

(answers on page 233)

Beheaded words

To behead a word, you chop off the first letter. Sometimes, when you do this, you get a brand-new word.

Here's a puzzle that gives you clues to words that change into other words when they're beheaded. For example—behead the word that means the opposite of closed, and you'll get the word that means a place where pigs are kept, or a tool to write with. The word is *open*. When you behead it, you get *pen*.

Ready? Go.

1. Behead the word that means "not fast" and you'll get the word that means "not high."

2. Behead the word that means "a sandy place by water" and you'll get the word that means "every single one."

3. Behead the word that's the name of a black bird and you'll get the word for what you do to make a small boat move.

4. Behead the word for what you think with and you'll get the word for falling water.

5. Behead the word for a scare and you'll get the word that's the opposite of wrong.

6. Behead the word that means "tidy" and you'll get the word for what you want to do at lunchtime.

Here are some harder beheading puzzles.

7. Behead the word that means "hard work" and you'll get the word for something cars need.

8. Behead the word for a precious metal and you'll get the word for something that has been around a long time.

9. Behead the word for a tool that helps you reach a high place and you'll get the name of a poisonous snake.

10. Behead the word for a tool that's used to smooth wood and you'll get the word for a small road.

11. Behead the word that means "to make a hole" and you'll get the word for the material that metal comes from.

12. Behead the word that means "sleep" and you'll get the word that means "wood for building."

(answers on page 233)

Opposites

What's the opposite of *cold? Hot*, of course.
See if you can think of the opposite for each of
these words. Each opposite is *one* word.

1. more

2. new

3. first

4. ahead

5. wet

6. high

7. far

8. early

Here are some more words for which to find opposites. *But*, each opposite must be a word that begins with the letter *s*.

1. crooked
2. happy
3. dull
4. hard
5. dangerous
6. weak
7. calm
8. quick

(answers on page 233)

A wordy dinosaur

Have you ever tried to see how many words you could make using the letters in just one word? For example, using the four letters in the little word **door,** you can make four other words: **do, or, rod,** and **odor.**

The word dinosaur has twice as many letters as door, but you can make a lot more than just twice as many words from them. It's possible to make at least 50 different words from the letters in **dinosaur!**

See how many words you can make. If you can get from 40 to 50, you're a Supergenius, Top Grade! From 30 to 39 makes you a Genius, Junior Class. From 20 to 29, you're a Whizzbang. And from 10 to 19, you're Pretty Smart.

(answers on page 234)

Changeover

Changeover is a game in which you change a word, one letter at a time, until you have a word that means the opposite of the word you started with. However, each time you change a letter, you must have a *real* word. Here's how to change **some** to **none** in three moves.

1. Change **some** to **come** by changing **s** to **c**.

2. Change **come** to **cone** by changing **m** to **n**.

3. Change **cone** to **none** by changing **c** to **n**.

And so, you've gone from some to none—a complete changeover! Now, try these changeovers on your own.

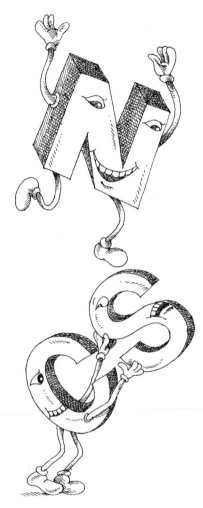

1. Change **glee** to **glum** in two moves.

2. Change **hill** to **vale** in three moves.

3. Change **more** to **less** in four moves.

4. Change **cold** to **heat** in four moves.

5. Change **hard** to **soft** in six moves.

(answers on page 234)

Strange lands

Five children who were traveling with their parents met at an airport. Although they all came from different countries, they found they all spoke the same language. But, just for fun, each child scrambled up the name of his or her country so the others would have to figure out what the real name was.

- Joe said he was from Andaca.

- Gail came from Duneti Testas.

- Molly was from Clonstad.

- Juanita came from an island called Turpeo Crio.

- Peter proudly stated he was from Tiasalura.

By rearranging the letters of each name, you can find out where each child was really from.

(answers on page 235)

A test for poets

Are you a poet—and don't know it? To find
out, see if you can fill in the right word in the
blank space in each of these little poems. But
remember, the words must not only rhyme,
they must also make sense.

1. I eat my peas with honey.
   I've done it all my life.
   It makes the peas taste funny,
   but they can't slide off my _____.

2. There was an old man from Peru,
   Who dreamed he was eating his shoe.
      He awoke in a fright,
      In the middle of the night,
   And found it was perfectly _____.

3. A centipede with thirty feet
   To himself said, "I refuse
   To spend the money I know it will take
   To buy myself new _____."

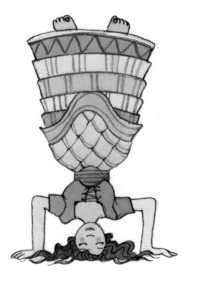

4. There was a young lady of Crete
   Who was most exceedingly neat.
      When she got out of bed,
      She stood on her head,
   To make sure of not soiling her _____.

(answers on page 235)

Put-together words

A lot of words are made out of sounds that are actually *other* words—short words that usually have nothing to do with the word they help to make. For example, *car*, a vehicle, and *pet*, a tame, owned animal, form the word *carpet*, a floor covering.

Here are clues for pairs of short words that can be put together to form other words. All the short words are words you know, although some of the words they make may be new to you.

1. Put together a word that's the name of part of your head and a word that means "a baby bird's home." You'll get a word that means "firm and serious."

2. Put together a word that's the name for part of a book and a word that's the name of an insect. You'll have a word that means "a showy spectacle or parade."

3. Put together a word that means "a small bed" and a word that's the name of a measure of weight. You'll have the name of a kind of cloth.

4. Put together a word that's the name of a cooking tool and a word that means "an attempt." You'll have the name of a small room where food is kept.

5. Put together a word that's the name of a head covering and a word that means the amount of space a thing takes up. You'll have a word that means "to overturn."

(answers on page 235)

Hidden words

Hidden in the next sentence is the name of a piece of furniture.

March air is often quite chilly.

Did you find it? The word is *chair*. It's made up of the *ch* in Mar*ch* followed by the word *air*.

In each of the sentences below is hidden the name of a thing you would probably want to take along on a picnic. Each thing is something to eat.

1. You can pick less fruit by hand than you can with a machine.

2. "There are two cats up in a tree," cried Jan.

3. Frank sings alto in the church choir.

4. Ants cannot eat wood, but termites can.

5. The college will enroll students in the fall.

(answers on page 235)

Rearranged words

In each of the sentences below there is one word that can be changed into a different word by rearranging the letters. Each sentence makes sense as it now is. But, if you can find the right word to change, the sentence will take on a new meaning.

For example: "We'll have to walk around this little loop of water," said Bob. The word that can be changed is *loop*. Perhaps there *could* be a *loop* of water formed by a tiny stream, so the sentence makes sense. But, when you change *loop* to *pool*, the sentence becomes more meaningful.

1. "I got a sore from that thorny bush," announced Mary.

2. "I have to put my hoses in the closet," called Jerry.

3. If you prod a drinking glass, it will probably break.

4. "Hear that low hooting in the woods?" asked Brian.

5. Church bells often seem to sound as if they're leaping for joy.

6. A fox crouched beside a rail in the forest.

7. "I saw a reed beside the river," said Jane.

(answers on page 236)

The Ongloti language

Can you read Ongloti? You can if you are reading this!

English is full of different letter combinations with the same sounds. The *o* in *women* sounds like the *i* in *win*. And the *ti* in *station* sounds like the *sh* in *shadow*. So, if you spell *English* with the *o* from *women* for the two *i* sounds and the *ti* from *station* for the *sh* sound, you get *Ongloti!*

Here are some other letter combinations and their sounds: the *ei* in *neighbor* sounds like the *a* in *nay;* the *o* in *one* sounds like the *w* in *won;* the *gh* in *tough* sounds like the *f* in *muff,* and the *or* in *work* sounds like the *ir* in *sir.* Keeping these in mind, can you figure out the following Ongloti words? There is a hint with each one.

1. oond   It can move things.

2. tielgh   You put things on it.

3. gheid   This often happens to clothes.

4. ghorst   It's number one.

(answers on page 236)

The two scientists

A scientist was looking through a telescope. Suddenly she turned to another scientist who stood nearby and exclaimed, "No more stars!"

What kind of scientists were they? You can find out by rearranging the letters in the words the scientist said.

(answer on page 237)

What's for breakfast?

In the country of Injuh, a man walked into a restaurant and sat down at a table. A waitress came over to him.

"FUNEM?" asked the man.

"SVFM," replied the waitress.

"FUNEX?" asked the man.

"SVFX," said the waitress.

"OK," said the man. "LFMNX."

Do you know what they said to each other?

(answer on page 237)

The pup's tale

A number of words in English read the same backwards as forwards. Such a word, for example, is *toot*. Another is *bib*, the cloth a baby wears under its chin when it eats.

A word that reads the same backwards or forwards is called a palindrome (PAL ihn drohm). See how many palindromes you can find in the following story:

The police had been called. The Smiths' family pet, a collie pup, had been stolen!

"Sis took him for a walk, at noon," said Mom, pointing to her little girl. "She stopped to buy a bottle of pop. When she turned around, the dog was gone."

The little girl was crying bitterly. Tears poured from each eye, and her face was redder than a radish.

"I wonder who did such a deed?" muttered the policeman. "I'll level with you; only a real dud would steal from such a tiny tot!"

"Wow!" Dad suddenly cried. "Look!"

There in the yard was the dog. It hadn't been stolen at all, just lost. And it had found its way home like an airplane following a radar signal!

(answer on page 237)

The secret agent and the code

You're a secret agent for your country and you've just captured an enemy agent! When you searched him, you found a code message that he had just decoded. It looked like this:

yjgp yknn vjga cvvcei
When will they attack

The enemy wants to know when your side is going to attack. You know that the attack will be made tonight. If you can send the enemy a message in their own code, telling them that the attack will be made tomorrow, they won't be ready when the attack really takes place!

Can you figure out how the enemy code works? Can you write the word *tomorrow* in their code?

(answer on page 238)

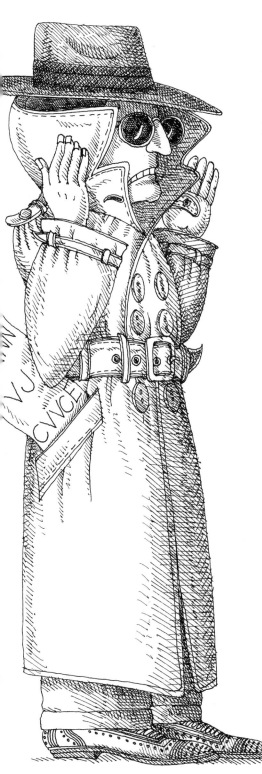

All kinds of codes

Here are some secret messages to decode. Once you've figured out how each code works, you can use it with your friends.

1. In this message, numbers are obviously used for letters. Here's a hint: everything is in the proper order.

   4 5 3 15 4 9 14 7   9 19   6 21 14

2. Look very carefully at this message:

   ITI SALLIN HO WYO ULOO KATIT

3. The clue for this message is: *backwards.*

   GSV ZOKSZYVG RH GFIMVW ZILFMW

4. This one is much harder, because you have to decode it twice. Here's a hint: This code combines two of the other codes. After you decode it once, look at it carefully.

   HKZ XVWW RUUV IVMGO BZMWYZ
   XPDZ IWH

   (answers on page 238)

What's in a name?

There are often hidden words in people's names. Here are some riddles about names with hidden words in them. Each riddle asks a question about the person, and the answer is always, "Because there's a, or an, *(the hidden word)* in his name." For example, a riddle about the name EARL might be: "Why can EARL hear so well?" Answer—"Because there's an EAR in his name (**EARL**)." See how it works?

1. Why is JANICE always cold?

2. Why is MILTON so heavy?

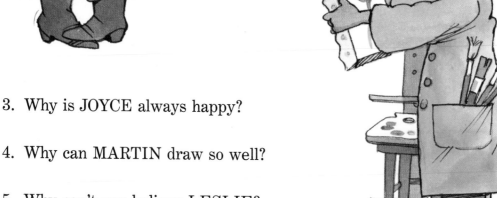

3. Why is JOYCE always happy?

4. Why can MARTIN draw so well?

5. Why can't you believe LESLIE?

6. Why doesn't CHRISTOPHER ever finish things?

7. Why doesn't RACHEL feel well?

8. Why can't you trust PATRICK?

9. Why can JANET catch fish so easily?

10. Why should EDWARD be a soldier?

11. Why does CHARLOTTE have so much of everything?

12. Why does STEWART always have plenty to eat?

(answers on page 239)

Animal, vegetable, mineral

Have you ever played the game called "Animal, Vegetable, or Mineral"? One person thinks of something that's animal, vegetable, or mineral. Then another person tries to find what it is by asking twenty questions.

Here's a different kind of animal, vegetable, mineral game. It is made up of twelve scrambled words. Four words are the names of things that belong to the animal kingdom, four belong to the vegetable kingdom, and four belong to the mineral kingdom. (Minerals are the lifeless things that come out of the earth, such as metals, rocks, and jewels.) The names aren't in any order. There's a clue with each, to help you figure out what it is. But—the clues are tricky!

1. NOFWESRUL
   It likes sunshine.

2. DALREEM
   It's bright green.

3. YISAD
   It lives in meadows.

4. BLUEBEMEB
   You may find one in your backyard.

5. OPREDLA
   It's orange and black.

6. TAINREG

You see it on many buildings.

7. DODMINA

Some people say it's their best friend.

8. HYNTOP

It's sometimes in trees.

9. PEALP

It's hard and red.

10. LUTTER

It has a hard shell.

11. PROCEP

It's shiny orange at first, but turns
brown as it gets old.

12. BERBRU

Cars roll down the road on it.

(answers on page 239)

Word breakdown

To play this game, you start with a word, take away one letter, and make a new word out of the letters left. Then, take a letter out of that word, and make still another word with the letters that are left. Keep doing this until you have only a one-letter word—such as A or I—left.

For example, start with the word MAPLE. Take away the E and rearrange the M, A, P, and L to make the word PALM. Then, take away the L to make MAP. Next, drop the P and make AM. And, finally, take away the M and you're left with the word A.

Now, try it with these words.

ORANGE   STREAM
PARTED   RETAIN
NAILED   RELATE

(answers on page 239)

Turnaround words (page 206)

1. ten—net
2. pan—nap
3. now—won
4. tool—loot
5. live—evil
6. liar—rail

Beheaded words (page 208)

1. slow; low
2. beach; each
3. crow; row
4. brain; rain
5. fright; right
6. neat; eat

More beheadings

7. toil; oil
8. gold; old
9. ladder; adder
10. plane; lane
11. bore; ore
12. slumber; lumber

Opposites (page 210)

1. more—less
2. new—old
3. first—last
4. ahead—behind
5. wet—dry
6. high—low
7. far—near
8. early—late

Opposites beginning with s

1. crooked—straight
2. happy—sad
3. dull—sharp
4. hard—soft
5. dangerous—safe
6. weak—strong
7. calm—stormy
8. quick—slow

Answers

A wordy dinosaur (page 213)

Here, in alphabetical order, are 50 words you can make using the letters in **dinosaur.** It is possible to make even more words, but most of them are not very common.

adorn[1]	don[5]	nod	rind[10]	sin
aid	dour[6]	nor	road	sir
air	drain	oar	roan[11]	so
an	dun[7]	on	rod	soar[13]
and	duo[8]	or	ruin	sod[14]
as	in	our	run	soda
dais[2]	ion[9]	raid	sad	son
darn[3]	iron	rain	said	sour
din[4]	is	ran	sand	sun
do	no	rid	sari[12]	us

1. Adorn means "to decorate."
2. A dais is a raised platform.
3. Darn means "to mend."
4. A din is a loud noise.
5. Don means "to put on."
6. Dour means "gloomy."
7. Dun is a dull, grayish-brown color.
8. A duo is two; a pair.
9. An ion is an atom or a particle with an electric charge.
10. The rind is the outer covering of a fruit.
11. Roan is a yellowish or brownish color sprinkled with gray or white.
12. A sari is a long piece of cotton or silk that is worn as a kind of dress.
13. Soar means "to fly at a great height or to fly upward."
14. Sod is grass-covered earth.

Changeover (page 214)

1. Change **glee** to **glue** and **glue** to **glum.**
2. Change **hill** to **hall; hall** to **hale** (which means healthy); and **hale** to **vale** (a small valley).
3. Change **more** to **lore** (stories about a certain subject); **lore** to **lose; lose** to **loss;** and **loss** to **less.**
4. Change **cold** to **hold; hold** to **held; held** to **head;** and **head** to **heat.**
5. Change **hard** to **card; card** to **cart; cart** to **part; part** to **port; port** to **sort;** and **sort** to **soft.**

Strange lands (page 215)

Andaca is Canada.
Duneti Testas is the United States.
Clonstad is Scotland.
Turpeo Crio is Puerto Rico.
Tiasalura is Australia.

A test for poets (page 216)

1. knife—to rhyme with life
2. true—to rhyme with shoe
3. shoes—to rhyme with refuse
4. feet—to rhyme with neat

Put together words (page 218)

1. ear + nest = earnest—firm and serious
2. page + ant = pageant—a showy spectacle
3. cot + ton = cotton—a kind of cloth
4. pan + try = pantry—a small room
5. cap + size = capsize—overturn

Hidden words (page 220)

1. Pickles. You will *pick les*s fruit by hand than you can with a machine.
2. Catsup. "There are two *cats up* in a tree," cried Jan.
3. Salt. Frank sing*s alt*o in the church choir.
4. Butter. Ants cannot eat wood, *but ter*mites can.
5. Rolls. The college will en*roll* students in the fall.

Answers

Rearranged words (page 221)

1. sore—rose You probably could get a *sore* from a thorny bush if you pricked yourself on a thorn. But what Mary really got from the thorny bush was a *rose*.
2. hoses—shoes Some people might keep *hoses* in a closet, but what Jerry was putting there was his *shoes*.
3. prod—drop A *prod*, or push, probably wouldn't cause a glass to break, but if you *drop* it, it would surely shatter.
4. low—owl If you were to hear *low* hooting in a woods, it would probably be an *owl* doing the hooting.
5. leaping—pealing Church bells may seem to sound as if they're *leaping* for joy. But we call the sound that church bells make *pealing*.
6. rail—lair There might well be a *rail* in a forest, but a fox would be more likely to crouch beside a *lair*, which is the name for an animal's hiding place.
7. reed—deer A *reed* could grow beside a river, but reeds grow in big clusters, not just one. What Jane saw was a *deer*.

The Ongloti language (page 222)

1. oond—wind: The *w* sound is the *o* from *one* and the *i* sound is the *o* from *women*.
2. tielgh—shelf: The *sh* sound is the *ti* from *station* and the *f* sound is the *gh* from *tough*.
3. gheid—fade: The *f* sound is the *gh* from *tough* and the *a* sound is the *ei* from *neighbor*.
4. ghorst—first: The *f* sound is the *gh* from *tough* and the *ur* sound is the *or* from *work*.

The two scientists (page 223)

The letters in "No more stars" can be rearranged to make the word *astronomers*. Astronomers are scientists who study the stars.

What's for breakfast? (page 224)

You can tell what the man and the waitress said to each other if you say each letter aloud *as a letter.*

The man says F-U-N-E-M. Say each letter aloud and you'll see that it sounds as if the man were saying "Have you any ham?"

The waitress says S-V-F-M, or "Yes we have ham."

The man says F-U-N-E-X, or "Have you any eggs?"

S-V-F-X, says the waitress, or "Yes we have eggs."

So, the man says, O-K. L-F-M-N-X, or "Okay. I'll have ham and eggs."

The pup's tale (page 225)

There are fifteen different palindromes in the story. In the order in which they appear, they are:

pup	mom	redder	level	wow
sis	pop	did	dud	dad
noon	eye	deed	tot	radar

Answers

The secret agent and the code (page 226)

yjgp yknn vjga cvvcei
when will they attack

In the first code word, **y** stands for **w**, and **j** stands for **h**. If you think about it, **y** is two letters after **w** in the alphabet. And **j** is two letters after **h.** So, the secret of the enemy code is simply to change each code letter to the letter that is two places after it in the alphabet. Thus **a** becomes **c,** **b** becomes **d,** and so on. In the enemy code, then, **tomorrow** is written **vqoqttqy.**

All kinds of codes (page 227)

1. Numbers are used for letters in proper alphabetical order. Thus, 1 is A, 2 is B, and so on. So, the message reads:

   4 5 3 15 4 9 14 7 9 19 6 21 14
   D E C O D I N G I S F U N

2. If you looked carefully, you saw that the message is made up of ordinary words that are just spaced differently:

   ITI SALLIN HO WYO ULOO KATIT
   IT IS ALL IN HOW YOU LOOK AT IT

3. The letters of the alphabet have been turned around so that A is Z, B is Y, and so on:

   GSV ZOKSZYVG RH GFIMVW ZILFMW
   THE ALPHABET IS TURNED AROUND

4. If you realized that this, too, is a backwards alphabet, as in (3), you decoded it and got:

   HKZ XVWW RUUV IVMGO BZMWYZ XPZD IWH
   SPA CEDD IFFE RENTL YANDBA CKWA RDS
   Then, if you looked at it carefully, as the clue suggested, you saw that it was just ordinary words spaced differently, as in (2).

   SPA CEDD IFFE RENTL YANDBA CKWA RDS
   SPACED DIFFERENTLY AND BACKWARDS

Answers

What's in a name? (page 228)

1. Because there's ICE in her name (JANICE)
2. Because there's a TON in his name (MILTON)
3. Because there's JOY in her name (JOYCE)
4. Because there's ART in his name (MARTIN)
5. Because there's a LIE in her name (LESLIE)
6. Because there's a STOP in his name (CHRISTOPHER)
7. Because there's an ACHE in her name (RACHEL)
8. Because there's a TRICK in his name (PATRICK)
9. Because there's a NET in her name (JANET)
10. Because there's WAR in his name (EDWARD)
11. Because there's a LOT in her name (CHARLOTTE)
12. Because there's STEW in his name (STEWART)

Animal, vegetable, mineral (page 230)

1. NOFWESRUL—SUNFLOWER (vegetable)
2. DALREEM—EMERALD (mineral)
3. YISAD—DAISY (vegetable)
4. BLUEBEMEB—BUMBLEBEE (animal)
5. OPREDLA—LEOPARD (animal)
6. TAINREG—GRANITE (mineral)
7. DODMINA—DIAMOND (mineral)
8. HYNTOP—PYTHON (animal)
9. PEALP—APPLE (vegetable)
10. LUTTER—TURTLE (animal)
11. PROCEP—COPPER (mineral)
12. BERBRU—RUBBER (vegetable)

Word breakdown (page 232)

ORANGE	PARTED	NAILED	STREAM	RETAIN	RELATE
RANGE	RATED	LINED	MEATS	TRAIN	LATER
RANG	TEAR	DINE	SEAT	RAIN	LATE
RAN	TEA	DIN	SAT	RAN	ATE
AN	AT	IN	AT	AN	AT
A	A	I	A	A	A

Many people like puzzles that use numbers. In other words, arithmetic puzzles. However, these puzzles are nothing like the plain old arithmetic problems you do for homework. Many of these puzzles are really jokes and tricks—arithmetricks! They're fun!

You'll need a pencil and paper for most of these puzzles, of course. And you'll have to know how to do some addition, subtraction, and multiplication. But, most of all, you must read *carefully* and use common sense.

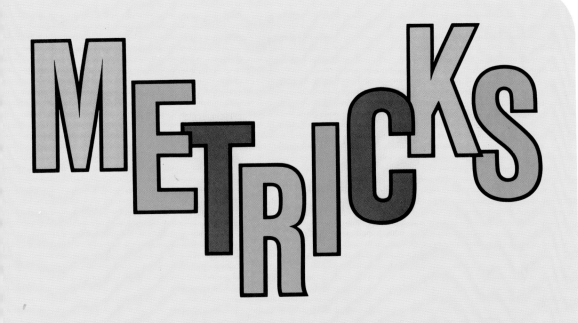

Many of these puzzles are easier than they seem, but they are tricky.

Some of the puzzles ask you to figure out how many of something somebody *started* with. But all you are told is how many they finished with. Here's an important hint for solving such puzzles: work *backwards*. That is, take the last number the puzzle gives and start subtracting or adding as needed. In this way, you can work back to the starting number.

Nimble numbers

1. When you add 10 to 100, you get 110. When you multiply 100 by 10, you get 1,000—a lot more. But what number makes a larger number when you *add* it to 100 than when you multiply it by 100?

2. What three numbers make the same number when they are multiplied as when they are added?

3. How can you make three 1's equal 12?

   1 1 1

4. How can you make four 7's equal 78?

   7 7 7 7

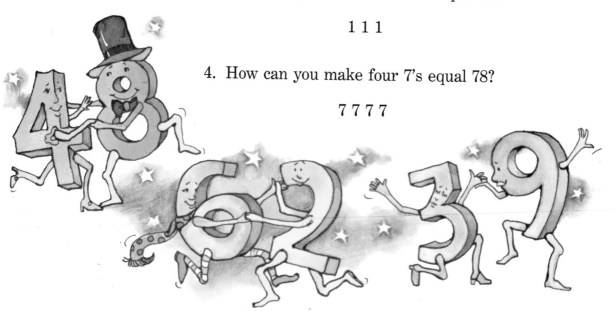

5. How much is double one-half of three-quarters?

(answers on page 265)

Careful, now!

1. Take a quick guess—how much is

$$10 \times 10 \times 10 \times 10 \times 10 \times 0$$

2. Jackie walked downtown from her house in one hour and fifteen minutes. Coming home, she didn't walk any faster and didn't take any short cuts. But it took her only 75 minutes. How was this possible?

3. It had been a beautiful, sunny day. But that night, at midnight, a man bet his wife that it wouldn't be sunny in 72 hours. As it turned out, he was right. How did he know?

4. You're very sleepy, so you decide to go to bed at 8:30. But you don't want to sleep too late the next day, so you set the alarm clock for 9:00 in the morning. How many hours of sleep will you get?

(answers on page 265)

The garage sale

Mrs. Wuggins went to a garage sale in her neighborhood. She bought an old lamp and a handmade rug. She paid a total of $5.25 for both of these things. The rug cost 25 cents more than the lamp. How much did each thing cost?

(answers on page 265)

The snail's pace

A snail began to climb straight up a wall. The wall was made of bricks and was exactly 24 bricks high. The snail climbed up three bricks each day. But each night it slid back two bricks.

How many days did it take the snail to reach the top of the wall?

(answers on page 266)

The explorers

Two explorers, a man and a woman, were
making their way through a thick jungle.
When they had to wade through a river, many
of their food packages were spoiled. They
divided the remaining packages into two equal
shares and continued on their way.

By the time the explorers reached
civilization, each one had eaten five food
packages. The total number of packages left
was the same number each explorer had
started with.

How many food packages had the explorers
divided?

(answer on page 266)

The two hippos

There were once two hippos who lived in the same lake in Africa. One was afraid she was much too fat. The other thought she was too thin. One day, they decided to weigh themselves.

Their combined weights came to 8,100 pounds (3,645 kilograms). The fat hippo weighed exactly twice as much as the thin hippo. How much did each hippo weigh?

(answers on page 266)

The antique clocks

Mrs. Bedelia Gackenbammer owns two very old antique clocks. One clock doesn't work at all. The other runs, but it loses 75 seconds (a minute and a quarter) every half hour.

If both clocks are set at twelve o'clock midnight on a Sunday, which one will show the right time most often during the next ten days?

(answer on page 267)

The Klucksburg clock

The town clock of Klucksburg strikes each hour with a deep *bong*. Each bong lasts one second. The time between two bongs is one-fourth of a second. It takes the clock six seconds to strike five o'clock. How long does it take it to strike nine o'clock?

(answer on page 267)

What time is it?

One hour ago, it was as long after one o'clock in the afternoon as it was before one o'clock in the morning. What time is it now?

(answer on page 267)

Crossed hands

There are twelve hours and two minutes in the period of time from one minute before twelve at night to one minute after twelve noon. How many times will a clock's big hand move across the little hand during that time?

(answer on page 268)

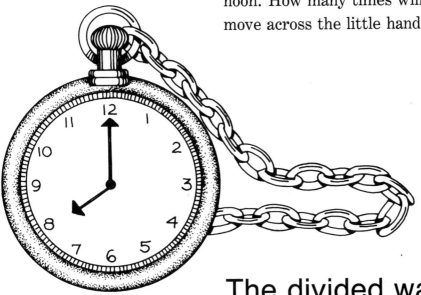

The divided watch

Lay two toothpicks across the face of this watch so as to divide it into three parts—and in such a way that the numbers in each part add up to 26.

(answer on page 268)

The three robbers

Long ago in England, there was a gang of three robbers. The leader was a big, broad man known as Tall Tam. One of the other robbers was a very small person called Wee Robin. The third robber was a middle-sized man who was known as John o' the Moor.

One day, the three robbers hid in a forest. When a pair of travelers came along, the robbers sprang out at them. They took all the travelers' money—many silver coins. Then the robbers went to their hideout to divide the money.

Because he was the biggest, and the others were afraid of him, Tall Tam took half the coins, plus one. Because John o' the Moor was bigger than Wee Robin, he took half of the remaining coins, plus one. This left Wee Robin with four silver coins.

How many coins did the robbers take from the group of travelers?

(answer on page 268)

Generous Nancy

Nancy had seven cookies. She was a generous person, so she gave half of what she had, plus half a cookie, to her baby sister. Then she gave half of what was left, plus half a cookie, to her little brother. She kept half of what was left, plus half a cookie, for herself.

How many cookies did each person get?

(answers on page 268)

Susan's grandma

Susan is a third as old as her mother, who is
five years younger than Susan's father.
Susan's grandmother is twice as old as
Susan's father. Susan is ten. How old is her
grandmother?

(answer on page 269)

Busy ants

Many kinds of ants make underground nests. The nests often have many tunnels leading up to the surface. Ant workers scurry in and out of these tunnels. Some go out to look for food. Others come back with food they have found.

Let's say that one ant nest has three tunnels leading up to the surface. Three worker ants are out looking for food. They all come back at the same time. How many different ways can they go into the nest, each using a different tunnel?

(answer on page 269)

A square triangle

The numbers 3, 6, and 10 are sometimes called triangular numbers. That's because, if you show them as balls, you can arrange each group of balls in the shape of a triangle:

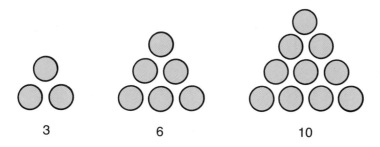

3   6   10

The numbers 4, 9, and 16 are sometimes called square numbers. That's because, if you show them as balls, the balls can be arranged in the shape of a square:

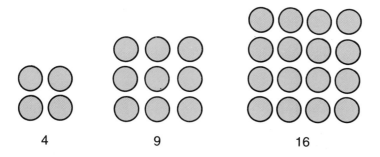

4   9   16

Many other numbers (past 2) can also be shown as either triangles or squares. But some numbers are both. What is the lowest number that can be shown as *both* a triangle and a square?

(answer on page 269)

The bottle game

A girl went to a carnival. She saw a booth where people were throwing balls at bottles. Six bottles were lined up in a row. There was a number on each bottle. For twenty-five cents the girl could throw three balls. If she knocked down three bottles whose numbers totaled exactly 50, she could win a bicycle!

The numbers on the bottles were

15 13 9 19 12 18

Which three bottles does the girl need to knock down to make a score of exactly 50?

(answer on page 269)

15 13 9 19 12 18

WIN A BICYCLE
SCORE 50 POINTS

Upside-down years

The year 1961 was special in a rather odd way. The number 1961 reads the same way upside down as it does right side up. And, a little more than a hundred years ago, there was another upside-down year—1881.

See if you can figure out what the next upside-down year will be. Remember, it has to look exactly the same upside down as it does right side up.

(answer on page 269)

The Dobbs children

The Dobbs children were all out playing in their backyard. All their pet dogs and cats were in the yard with them. When Mr. Dobbs looked out the window, he saw, counting children, dogs, and cats, seven heads and twenty-two legs. How many children were playing in the yard?

(answer on page 270)

Growing younger?

Ellen's father is now five times older than she is. But he told her that in five more years, he'll only be *three* times as old as she'll be then. Is this possible? (You'll have to do a little arithmetic to find out.)

(answer on page 270)

The stolen banana

A small monkey stole a banana from a big
monkey and ran away with it. The small
monkey ran 14 steps before the big monkey
saw what had happened. Then the big monkey
chased the small one. For every 10 steps the
little monkey ran, the big monkey took 5
steps, but these 5 steps were equal to 12 of
the little monkey's steps.

How many steps will the little monkey take
before the big monkey catches up to it?

(answer on page 270)

Sharp Ears and Striped Tail

Two raccoons, named Sharp Ears and Striped Tail, had gathered two hundred ears of ripe corn. Before they could store it away for the winter, they had to peel the leaves off each ear, which is called shucking. Sharp Ears could shuck thirty ears of corn in an hour. Striped Tail could shuck twenty ears in an hour. How long did it take them to shuck all two hundred ears of corn?

(answer on page 271)

Bread for wood

Three goblins, named Snurf, Snagga, and Guff, lived in a clearing in a woods. Each goblin had his own small but cozy house.

One cold winter day, Snurf and Snagga went out to get firewood. Guff stayed home to bake bread. The three had agreed to divide the firewood evenly. Guff would pay for his share with loaves of bread.

Snurf found a long log. He cut it into five pieces, each as long as he was. Snagga found a shorter log. He cut it into three pieces, each as long as he was. Inasmuch as the goblins

were exactly the same size, the pieces of wood were all the same size.

Snurf and Snagga brought their wood home. They saw they couldn't divide eight pieces three ways, of course. But they cut each piece into three pieces, so that there were twenty-four altogether—making eight for each of them. Guff gave them eight loaves of bread to pay for his eight pieces.

However, Snurf and Snagga disagreed on how to divide the loaves. Snurf felt he should get more than Snagga because he had brought home more wood. How can Snurf and Snagga divide the loaves fairly?

(answer on page 271)

Thirteen coins

Don asked his father for a dollar. "I have a lot of change, Don," his father said. He dumped a pile of coins on the table. "If you can find thirteen coins that add up to *exactly* one dollar (100 cents), you can have them."

There were several half dollars (50 cents) and quarters (25 cents) in the pile. And there were lots of dimes (10 cents) and nickels (5 cents) and pennies (1 cent). Don thought it would be easy to find thirteen coins that added up to exactly 100 cents. But he couldn't do it! Can you? (It *can* be done.)

(answer on page 271)

Nimble numbers (page 242)

1. The number 1. When you multiply 100 by 1, you get 100. But when you add 1 to 100, you get 101.
2. The numbers 1, 2, and 3: $1 + 2 + 3 = 6$ and $1 \times 2 \times 3 = 6$.
3. Arrange the three 1's this way: $11 + 1 = 12$.
4. Arrange the four 7's this way: $77 + 7/7 = 78$. (7/7—seven-sevenths—is equal to 1.)
5. Double one-half of three-quarters is three-quarters. Twice one-half of any number is the whole number.

Careful, now! (page 243)

1. Any number, or group of numbers, multiplied by 0 equals 0.
2. It took Jackie the same amount of time both going and coming. One hour and fifteen minutes *is* 75 minutes.
3. The man knew it wouldn't be sunny in 72 hours because 72 hours from midnight is midnight three days later—and, of course, there's no sun at midnight.
4. If you fall asleep right at 8:30, you'll get only half an hour of sleep. The alarm will ring at 9:00, one-half hour later.

The garage sale (page 244)

Subtract the 25 cents difference from the total and get $5.00. Half of this is $2.50. So, Mrs. Wuggins paid $2.50 for the lamp and $2.75 for the rug.

Answers

The snail's pace (page 245)

It took the snail 22 days. If the snail climbs three bricks a day and slips back two bricks each night, it is actually gaining one brick a day. So, after 21 nights, the snail had climbed 21 bricks. The next day, it climbed the last three bricks and reached the top of the wall.

The explorers (page 246)

The explorers divided the remaining food packages equally. In other words, each explorer had *half* the packages.

When they got to civilization, the number of packages they had left equaled the number each had started with. So, if each started with half the packages, the number left must equal half of the total they divided.

If half the packages were left, the explorers must have eaten the other half. We know they each ate five, which would be a total of ten, or half of what they started with. So, half of the total number must be ten. Therefore, they divided twenty packages.

The two hippos (page 247)

The fat hippo weighs twice as much as the thin one. Thus, the thin hippo's weight must be one-third of the total, and the fat hippo's weight is two-thirds—twice as much. So, you can find each animal's weight by dividing the total weight by three. This will give you one-third of the total—the thin hippo's weight. Then, multiply that by two, and you have the fat hippo's weight.

The thin hippo weighed 2,700 pounds (1,215 kilograms) and the fat hippo weighed 5,400 pounds (2,430 kg).

The antique clocks (page 248)

The clock that doesn't work will show the right time twenty times during the next ten days—at twelve noon and twelve midnight each day. The clock that runs, but loses time, won't show the right time *at all* during the next ten days!

The clock that runs loses 75 seconds every half hour. This works out to one-half hour every twelve hours. Thus, at twelve noon on Monday, this clock will show eleven-thirty. At midnight Monday it will show eleven o'clock. And each day after that, it gets farther off.

This clock actually won't show the right time for twelve days. It will have lost twelve hours in twelve days, so it will finally show twelve o'clock at midnight on the twelfth day.

The Klucksburg clock (page 248)

It takes exactly eleven seconds for the clock to strike nine. There are nine one-second bongs. And, there are eight quarter-seconds, or a total of two seconds, between bongs.

What time is it? (page 249)

If you think carefully about what this puzzle says, you'll see that one hour ago the clock showed just as many hours *after* one o'clock in the afternoon as *before* one o'clock in the morning.

Thus, one hour ago the time must have been exactly *halfway* between one in the afternoon and one in the morning. There are twelve hours between one in the afternoon and one in the morning. Half of that is six hours, which is seven o'clock at night. If it were seven o'clock one hour ago, the time *now* is eight o'clock.

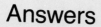

Answers

Crossed hands (page 249)

From one minute to twelve at night, to one minute after twelve noon, a clock's hands will cross thirteen times.

The divided watch (page 249)

Place the toothpicks as shown in the picture at the left. The numbers in each part total 26.

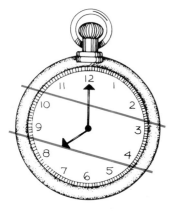

The three robbers (page 251)

You can solve this puzzle by working backwards. The little robber had four coins. The middle robber took half, plus one, of the coins left *after* the leader took his share. Therefore, the little robber's four coins must be one coin less than the half the middle robber took. So the half the middle robber took has to be five.

This means the middle robber had ten coins to take from. Those coins were left after the leader took half, plus one, of the total coins. So, the ten coins are one coin less than half of the total amount. Thus, half the total must be eleven. Then the total number of coins the robbers stole was twenty-two.

The leader took eleven coins (half of twenty-two) plus one, or twelve. This left ten coins. The middle robber took half of those, plus one, or six. This left the little robber with four.

Generous Nancy (page 252)

Nancy gave her baby sister half of the seven cookies, plus half a cookie. Half of seven is three and a half, and half a cookie makes four. So, the baby got four cookies, leaving Nancy three.

Nancy gave half of the three cookies, plus half a cookie, to her brother. Half of three is one and a half, plus a half makes two.

That leaves one cookie. Nancy kept half of what was left (half a cookie), plus half a cookie, so she got one cookie.

Answers

Susan's grandma (page 253)

Susan is ten, so if she is a third as old as her mother, her mother is thirty ($10 \times 3 = 30$). Susan's mother is five years younger than Susan's father, so he is thirty-five. If Susan's grandmother is twice as old as Susan's father, then the grandmother is seventy years old.

Busy ants (page 254)

There are six possible ways. Number the tunnels 1, 2, and 3. Call the ants A, B, and C. Then you can see how this works out:

	Tunnel					Tunnel		
Ways	1	2	3		Ways	1	2	3
(1)	A	B	C		(4)	C	A	B
(2)	A	C	B		(5)	B	C	A
(3)	B	A	C		(6)	C	B	A

A square triangle (page 255)

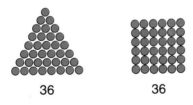

36   36

The bottle game (page 256)

She needs to knock down the bottles numbered 13, 19, and 18 to get a total of 50.

Upside-down years (page 258)

There won't be another upside-down year for more than four thousand years—not until the year 6009!

Answers

The Dobbs children (page 259)

Mr. Dobbs counted seven heads, so you know the number of dogs, cats, and children must add up to seven. And as the puzzle said there were dogs and cats, you know there must be *at least* two dogs and two cats. Four animals and three children would account for the seven heads Mr. Dobbs counted.

Two dogs and two cats, with four legs each, would account for sixteen legs ($4 \times 4 = 16$). Three children, with two legs each, accounts for six legs ($3 \times 2 = 6$). And $16 + 6 = 22$, the number of legs Mr. Dobbs counted. So there were three children playing in the back yard.

Growing younger? (page 259)

Pick any number for Ellen's age. Multiply it by five to get her father's age. Then add five to both numbers to see if one is now three times the other. It may take you several tries to find that if Ellen is five, her father has to be twenty-five, five times older. In five years, then, Ellen will be ten and her father will be thirty, or three times older.

The stolen banana (page 260)

The little monkey will be caught by its eighty-fourth step.

The little monkey starts out 14 steps ahead. Then the big monkey starts to chase it. As the little monkey runs 10 steps, the big monkey runs 5 steps that are equal to 12 of the little monkey's steps. So, at this point, the little monkey has run 24 steps and the big monkey is 12 steps behind.

From then on, for every 10 steps the little monkey takes, the big monkey gains two steps.

When the small monkey has run 34 steps, the big one is 10 steps behind. At 44 steps for the small monkey, the big one is 8 behind. When the little monkey has run 74 steps, the big one is only two behind. The big monkey will catch the little one after it has taken ten more steps.

Sharp Ears and Striped Tail (page 261)

Sharp Ears could shuck thirty ears an hour and Striped Tail could do twenty. That's fifty ears an hour. So, it took them four hours to shuck all two hundred ears ($4 \times 50 = 200$).

Bread for wood (page 262)

Snurf should get seven loaves and Snagga should get one loaf.

The five pieces of wood Snurf brought home were cut into fifteen pieces. Snurf kept eight pieces, which means he gave away seven. The three pieces of wood Snagga brought were cut into nine pieces. So, inasmuch as Snagga kept eight pieces, he gave away only one.

Thirteen coins (page 264)

There are several ways to get thirteen coins that equal 100 cents:

Coin	Value	No.	Value	No.	Value	No.	Value
half-dollar	50 cents	1	50	-	-	-	-
quarter	25 cents	-	-	-	-	1	25
dime	10 cents	2	20	7	70	7	70
nickel	5 cents	5	25	6	30	-	-
penny	1 cent	5	5	-	-	5	5
		13	100	13	100	13	100

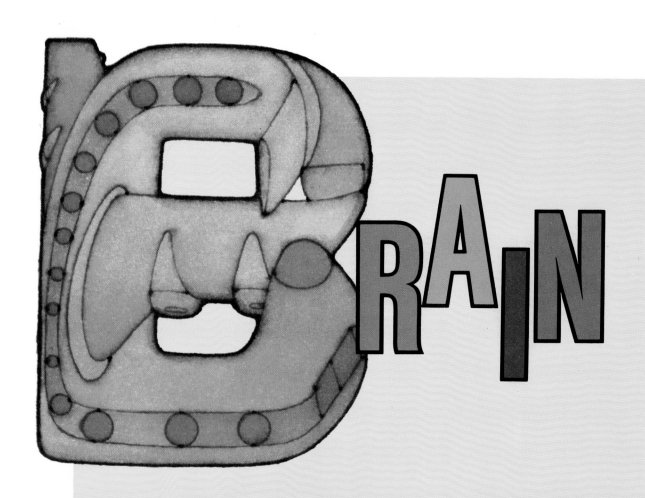

BUSTERS

These puzzles are just like some of the puzzles you've already met, except that they are harder. Some of them are simply trickier Arithmetricks, some are more ponderous Ponderers, some are twistier Brain Twisters. You go about solving them the same way you solved the other puzzles. However, you'll have to work a lot harder—but, of course, that's where the fun comes in!

Who earns the most?

Bill and Ellen had just begun work at their first jobs and were talking about them.

"I get paid $5,000 for the first six months," said Ellen. "Then my salary goes up $50 every six months from then on."

"My salary is $10,000 a year," Bill told her. "I get a $200 raise at the beginning of each year."

If they both keep working at their jobs for five years, who will earn the most money?

(answer on page 291)

What's the number?

A mother, father, and two children were driving from one city to another for a vacation. The car was moving at a speed of 55 miles (or 55 kilometers) an hour.

Suddenly, the father, who was driving, noticed something. "Look at the dial that shows how far we've come," he said. "It shows the number 11911. That number is the same backward as it is forward. That's unusual. I bet it will be a long time before the dial shows a number like that again!"

But he was wrong. Only two hours later, the dial showed another number that was also the same backward as it was forward. What was the number?

(answer on page 291)

Squirrels and nuts

Two squirrels named Chatter and Chitter were gathering nuts for winter. They had agreed to divide all the nuts they gathered into two equal shares.

Each squirrel gathered all the nuts he could find. Then the two got together to divide up the nuts. Unfortunately, squirrels aren't very good at arithmetic. It took them three tries to divide the nuts equally!

On the first try, Chatter gave Chitter as many nuts as Chitter already had. But that didn't make things even, so they tried again.

On the second try, Chitter gave back to Chatter as many nuts as Chatter now had. But that still didn't make things even.

On the third try, Chitter gave Chatter 10 more nuts. That made everything right, because now each one had 50 nuts.

How many nuts had each squirrel collected?

(answer on page 292)

The coin test

Long ago, people weighed things in a kind of scale called a balance. A balance is simply two pans, one hanging from each end of a long rod. The rod is balanced across a bar—like a teeter-totter. When an object is placed in each pan, the pan with the heaviest object dips down. If both objects weigh the same, the pans balance.

Once upon a time, in the city of Samarkand, a young girl went to a merchant to ask for a job. The merchant decided to test the young girl's cleverness. She showed the girl nine gold coins and a balance.

"These nine coins look exactly alike," said the merchant. "But one of them is a counterfeit. It isn't pure gold, so it does not weigh as much as the others.

"You could easily find the counterfeit coin by weighing all the coins, two at a time," the merchant continued. "If two coins balanced, you'd know they were both pure gold. If one was lighter than another, you'd know it was the counterfeit. But, to do that, you might have to use the balance as many as four times. Can you find the counterfeit coin using the balance only twice?"

How could the young girl do it?

(answer on page 292)

The five hobbyists

In a small town live five ladies who are close friends. Their names are: Ms. Schmidt, Ms. Rodriguez, Miss Fujimoto, Mrs. Kowalski, and Mrs. Robinson.

Each lady has a different hobby. One is a gardener. One makes pottery. One knits. One is a painter. One writes stories.

From the following six clues, can you tell which lady has which hobby?

1. Mrs. Kowalski doesn't care for gardening.

2. The gardener and Ms. Schmidt went to school together.

3. Mrs. Kowalski and Miss Fujimoto wear scarves that were made by the knitter.

4. Miss Fujimoto and the writer often have lunch with the gardener.

5. The gardener, the knitter, and Ms. Rodriguez have some of the vases made by the pottery maker.

6. Mrs. Kowalski asked Ms. Rodriguez if she thought the painter would do a portrait of her daughter.

(answers on page 293)

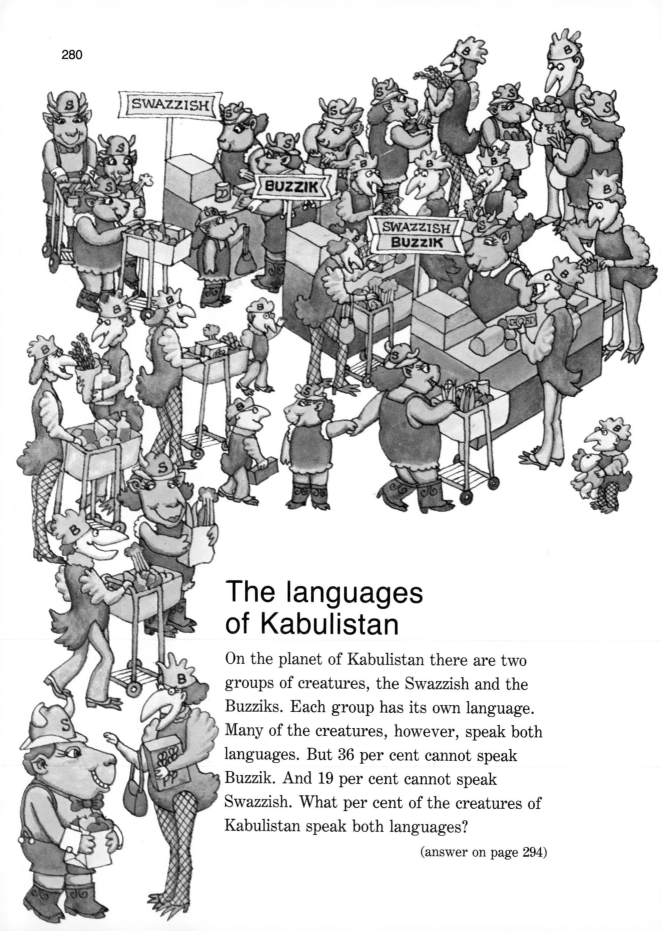

The languages of Kabulistan

On the planet of Kabulistan there are two groups of creatures, the Swazzish and the Buzziks. Each group has its own language. Many of the creatures, however, speak both languages. But 36 per cent cannot speak Buzzik. And 19 per cent cannot speak Swazzish. What per cent of the creatures of Kabulistan speak both languages?

(answer on page 294)

The flight to Los Angeles

Two women and a man were passengers on an airplane flying from Chicago to Los Angeles. These people happened to have the same last names as the pilot, the copilot, and the flight engineer on the plane. The names were Hirsch, Bruce, and Linden. But which one was the pilot, which one was copilot, and which one was the flight engineer?

Here are five clues to help you figure out their names:

1. Mrs. Hirsch was flying back to her home in Los Angeles.

2. The crew member named Bruce was married to the flight engineer's sister.

3. The passenger with the same name as the pilot was going on a two-week vacation.

4. The man with the same last name as the copilot lived in Chicago.

5. The passenger whose last name was Bruce was retired.

(answers on page 294)

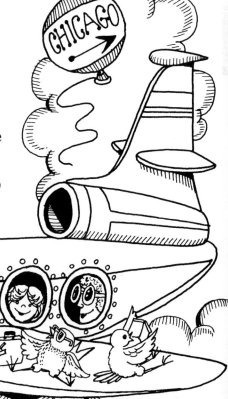

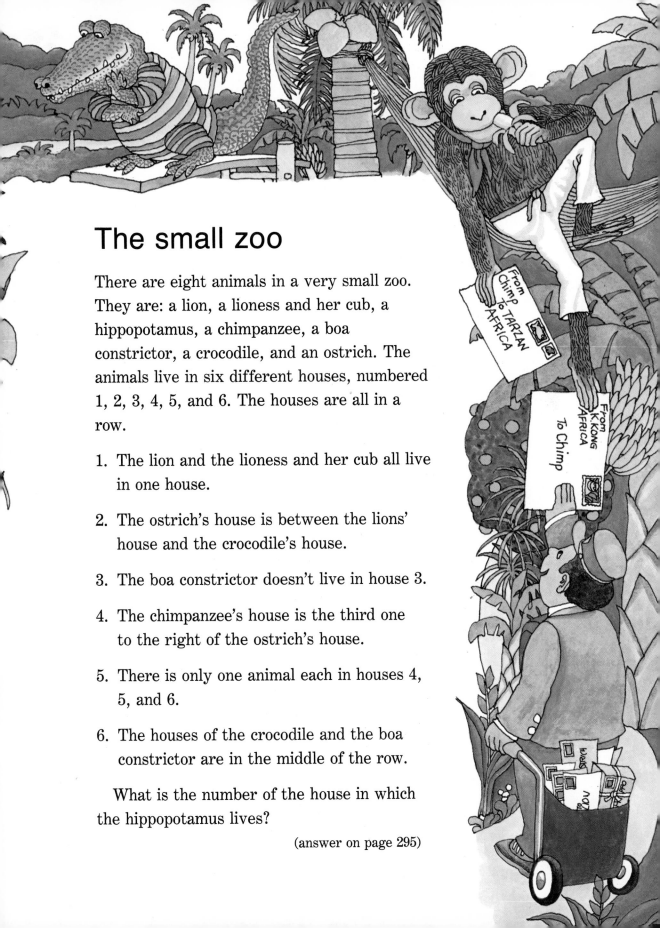

The small zoo

There are eight animals in a very small zoo. They are: a lion, a lioness and her cub, a hippopotamus, a chimpanzee, a boa constrictor, a crocodile, and an ostrich. The animals live in six different houses, numbered 1, 2, 3, 4, 5, and 6. The houses are all in a row.

1. The lion and the lioness and her cub all live in one house.

2. The ostrich's house is between the lions' house and the crocodile's house.

3. The boa constrictor doesn't live in house 3.

4. The chimpanzee's house is the third one to the right of the ostrich's house.

5. There is only one animal each in houses 4, 5, and 6.

6. The houses of the crocodile and the boa constrictor are in the middle of the row.

What is the number of the house in which the hippopotamus lives?

(answer on page 295)

Frank's folly

Two boys, Frank and Larry, were walking home from a candy store. They had just spent their whole allowances on candy!

Frank sighed. "I wish I had twice as much candy as I have now," he said.

"How much do you have?" asked Larry.

Frank told him. Larry, who was very good at arithmetic, thought for a while. Then he said, "We have to walk three more blocks to get home. So, I'll tell you what—at the end of each block, I'll give you enough of my candy so that you'll have twice as much as at the start of each block. But each time, you have to give me back eight pieces so that I'll have some, too. Is it a deal?"

It seemed like a great idea to Frank. "Sure!" he exclaimed.

At the end of the first block, Larry gave Frank enough candy so that he had twice what he started with. Frank then gave back eight pieces.

At the end of the second block, Larry doubled Frank's candy again. He got back eight pieces.

At the end of the third block, they did this again. But this time, when Frank gave back eight pieces—he had nothing left!

How many pieces of candy did Frank have to start with?

(answer on page 296)

The dull movie

A very dull movie was being shown at the
Cinema Theater one evening. The movie was
so bad that one-third of the audience left
during the first part of it. One-half of the rest
left during the middle part. And one-half of
those left in the theater walked out during
the last part. Only 25 people were in their
seats when the movie ended.

How many people were in the audience
when the movie began?

(answer on page 296)

The small round table

King Ondolph of Puggia was not as great a king as King Arthur of Britain. Ondolph commanded only six knights—Sir Pudno, Sir Mollix, Sir Baffin, Sir Coddle, Sir Morgid, and Sir Dollop. However, King Ondolph wanted to be as much like King Arthur as possible. So he had a round table built for his knights to sit at. (Of course, it was a rather small round table, for there were only six knights!)

When all six knights sat at the table, the strongest knight was across from Sir Coddle, who was to the right of Sir Baffin. Sir Pudno sat across from the fattest knight, and to the right of the strongest knight. The knight in red armor sat between Sir Coddle and the thin knight, and across from the knight who rode a white horse. And Sir Dollop sat to the right of the left-handed knight, across from the thin knight, and next to Sir Mollix.

From all this, can you figure out:

1. The name of the strongest knight?

2. The name of the knight in red armor?

3. The name of the left-handed knight?

4. The name of the thin knight?

5. The name of the fattest knight?

6. The name of the knight who rode a white horse?

(answers on page 298)

A nutty puzzle

Nicodemus Nubbs sold nuts. One day, Nicodemus went to town with a large basket that was full of nuts. He quickly found a customer—a lady bought half the nuts in his basket, plus half a nut!

A short while later, another customer hailed Nicodemus. This man bought half the nuts in the basket, plus half a nut.

Soon after, there was another customer—a little girl. She bought one-third of the nuts Nicodemus had left.

Nicodemus now had exactly one dozen nuts in his basket. All the nuts were whole, and all the nuts he had started with had been whole. Nicodemus hadn't had to cut any nuts in half when he made his sales.

How many nuts did he start with? How many nuts did each customer buy?

(answers on page 299)

The lunch bunch

Six children rode their bicycles to McMullin's Hamburger Restaurant for lunch.

1. Matt had what Mary Jo did, except that he did not have an ice-cream sundae.

2. Diana had what Brian had, plus a hamburger.

3. Gail had what Judy had, but without French fries.

4. Mary Jo had what Judy had, but she had pop instead of a milk shake.

5. Brian had the same things Matt did, except that he did not have a hamburger.

What did each child have for lunch?

(answers on page 300)

Fish stories

1. A girl carrying a fishing pole and a large fish she had just caught was walking by a lake. She met a man coming the other way.

   "Say, that's a whopper," said the man, pointing at the fish. "Have you had it weighed?"

   "Yep," said the girl. "It weighs ten pounds (4.5 kilograms) plus half its weight."

   How much did the fish weigh?

2. As the girl walked on, she met another man.

   "That's a good-sized fish," said the man. "How long is it?"

   "Well," said the girl, "the head is four inches (10 centimeters). The tail is as long as the head plus half the length of the body. And the body is exactly as long as the head and tail together."

   How long was the fish?

(answers on page 301)

Who earns the most? (page 274)

It seems as if Bill, with his yearly $200 raise should earn more. But Ellen will actually earn $50 a year more than Bill.

Bill gets his raise at the beginning of each year. So, he won't have a raise during his first year. He'll just make his $10,000 salary. But Ellen gets a $50 raise after her first six months. She earns $5,000 the first six months, and $5,050 the next six. That's a total of $10,050—which is $50 more than Bill will make.

At the start of his second year, Bill gets a $200 raise. He'll earn $10,200.

Ellen gets another $50 raise at the end of her second six months of work. So, her salary for the first six months of the second year will go up to $5,100. She gets another raise midway through the year, to $5,150. So, for her second year, she'll make $10,250 altogether. Again, that's $50 more than Bill will earn.

Ellen will always be $50 ahead of Bill. At the end of five years, she'll have earned $250 more than Bill.

Answers

What's the Number? (page 275)

The car was traveling at a speed of 55 miles (or 55 kilometers) an hour. Thus, in two hours it will go 110 miles (or 110 kilometers). Add 110 to 11911 and you'll get 12021, the new backward-forward number that showed on the dial.

Answers

Squirrels and nuts (page 276)

Inasmuch as the squirrels finished with 50 nuts each, you know, of course, that they started with a total of 100 nuts. To find out how many each squirrel had collected, you work backwards.

On the third try, Chitter gave Chatter 10 nuts and they both had 50. That means that *before* the third try, Chitter must have had 60 nuts and Chatter had 40.

On the second try, Chitter gave Chatter as many nuts as Chatter already had. This left Chitter with 60 and Chatter with 40. So, before this, Chatter must have had 20 nuts and Chitter 80.

Chitter had the 80 nuts after the first try, when Chitter gave him as many nuts as Chatter already had. So Chitter must have started with 40 nuts, and Chatter gave him 40 more to make 80. And if Chitter started with 40 nuts, Chatter must have started with 60.

The coin test (page 277)

The young girl must put three coins in each of the balance pans, setting the other three coins aside. If one pan sinks down, she will know that one of the coins in the other pan is a counterfeit. If the pans balance, she will know that the counterfeit is one of the three coins she set aside.

When the girl knows which group of coins includes the counterfeit, she can then put two of the coins in this group in the balance, one in each pan. She sets the other coin aside. If one of the coins in the balance is heavier, the other one is the counterfeit. If they balance, the coin she put aside is the counterfeit.

Thus, using the balance only twice, the young girl can find out which coin is the counterfeit.

The five hobbyists (page 278)

Clues 1, 2, and 4 tell us that the gardener cannot be Mrs. Kowalski, Ms. Schmidt, or Miss Fujimoto. Clue 5 reveals that Ms. Rodriguez isn't the gardener either. That leaves only Mrs. Robinson. She's the gardener.

Clue 3 tells us that neither Mrs. Kowalski nor Miss Fujimoto is the knitter. Clue 5 also shows that Ms. Rodriguez isn't the knitter. So, the only one left who can be the knitter is Ms. Schmidt.

From clue 5 we also know that Ms. Rodriguez isn't the pottery maker. Thus, she has to be either the painter or the writer. Clue 4 reveals that Miss Fujimoto isn't the writer, so she must be either the painter or pottery maker. As for Mrs. Kowalski, she might be the painter, the writer, or the pottery maker.

But clue 6 reveals that neither Mrs. Kowalski nor Ms. Rodriguez is the painter. Inasmuch as Ms. Rodriguez has to be either the painter or the writer, she is obviously the writer. With Mrs. Kowalski ruled out as both painter and writer, she must be the pottery maker. That leaves Miss Fujimoto as the painter.

So, the five hobbyists are:
- Mrs. Robinson, gardener
- Ms. Schmidt, knitter
- Ms. Rodriguez, writer
- Mrs. Kowalski, pottery maker
- Miss Fujimoto, painter.

Answers

Answers

The languages of Kabulistan (page 280)

We know that 36 per cent of the creatures speak only Swazzish. And 19 per cent speak only Buzzik. That's 55 per cent who speak only one language. This means that 45 per cent of the creatures speak both languages.

The flight to Los Angeles (page 281)

Clue 2 reveals that the flight engineer's name isn't Bruce. He has to be Hirsch or Linden.

Clue 3, together with clue 1, shows that the pilot's name can't be Hirsch. Clue 3 says the passenger with the same name as the pilot was going on a vacation. But clue 1 said that Mrs. Hirsch was going home—not on vacation. Thus, the pilot has to be either Bruce or Linden.

Clue 4 shows that the copilot can't be named Hirsch. The clue says the *man* with the same name as the copilot lived in Chicago. From clue 1, we know Mrs. Hirsch is a woman and that she lives in Los Angeles. So the copilot is either Bruce or Linden.

Clue 5 says that the person with the same name as the pilot is retired—in other words, does not have a job. Usually, a person takes a vacation *from* a job. Therefore, the person named Bruce, who is going on vacation, does not have the same name as the pilot. So, the pilot's name must be Linden. Bruce, then, is the copilot's name, and Hirsch is the name of the flight engineer.

The small zoo (page 283)

Clue 2 reveals that the ostrich's house is between two other houses. This means that the house of the ostrich can't be either house 1 or 6. It has to be 2, 3, 4, or 5.

Clue 3 indicates that the snake lives in house 1, 2, 4, 5, or 6.

Clue 4 says that the chimpanzee's house is the third one from the ostrich's house. The ostrich's house is known to be 2, 3, 4, or 5. But there can't be a third house after house 4 or 5 because that house would be 7 or 8, and there are only 6 houses. So, we know the ostrich lives in 2 or 3. The third house from 2 is 5, and the third from 3 is 6. The chimpanzee must live in 5 or 6.

Up to now, we have learned that:
- The boa constrictor lives in 1, 2, 4, 5, or 6.
- The ostrich lives in 2 or 3
- The chimpanzee lives in 5 or 6.

Clue 5 reveals there is only one animal each in houses 4, 5, and 6. We know that the lions are together, so they must live in 1, 2, or 3.

Clue 6 tells us the houses of the crocodile and the boa constrictor are in the middle of the row. Thus, they have to be houses 3 and 4, with 1 and 2 on one side, and 5 and 6 on the other. We know from clue 3 that the snake doesn't live in house 3, so he has to live in house 4. Then the crocodile must live in house 3.

Clue 2 tells us the ostrich's house is between the lions' house and the crocodile's house. We know that the ostrich lives in either house 2 or 3. As the crocodile lives in 3, the ostrich has to live in house 2. Therefore, the lions must live in 1.

The chimpanzee's house is the third one after the ostrich's house. The third house after house 2 is house 5. This leaves only house 6, which has to be the hippo's house.

Frank's folly (page 284)

To solve this puzzle, work backwards.

At the end of the third block, Frank gave Larry eight pieces of candy and had none left. The eight pieces were what Frank had after his candy had been doubled. Eight is four doubled. So, at the end of the third block Frank must have had four pieces.

$$4 \times 2 = 8 - 8 = 0$$

The four pieces were left after Frank gave *back* eight pieces at the end of the second block. Eight and four are twelve, so twelve pieces is what Frank had after Larry doubled Frank's candy. Twelve is six doubled. Thus, Frank had six pieces when he started down the second block.

$$6 \times 2 = 12 - 8 = 4$$

Those six pieces were left after Frank gave *back* eight pieces at the end of the first block. Eight and six are fourteen. Fourteen is what Frank had after his candy was doubled. Fourteen is seven doubled, so Frank started out with seven pieces of candy.

$$7 \times 2 = 14 - 8 = 6$$

The dull movie (page 285)

At the beginning of the movie, there were 150 people in the audience.

To get this answer, you have to work backwards from the number of people, 25, that were still in the theater when the movie ended.

You know that there were 25 people left after *half* the people walked out during the last part of the movie. As 25 is half of 50, there must have been 50 people in the theater when the last part of the movie began.

You know that half the people in the audience left during the middle part of the movie. Thus, the 50 people still there were the other half. So, there must have been 100 people when the middle part of the movie began.

You know that one-third of the whole audience left during the first part of the movie. Thus, the 100 people who sat through the middle part of the movie were *two-thirds* of the whole audience. If you divide 100 by 2 you will get 50, which is one-third of the *total* audience. Therefore, 50 people left during the first part of the movie, and 50 plus 100 is 150—the number of people in the audience when the movie began.

Answers

Answers

The small round table (page 286)

The best way to solve this puzzle is to draw a circle for the table and fill in names and places as the clues reveal them.

The first clue tells us the strongest knight was across from Sir Coddle, who was to the right of Sir Baffin. This gives us three positions.

The second clue says that Sir Pudno sat across from the fattest knight, and to the right of the strongest knight. This gives us two more positions.

Clue three tells us the knight in red armor sat between Sir Coddle and the thin knight. The only person who is between Coddle and someone else is Sir Baffin—so, he is the knight in red armor. And now we also know that as Sir Pudno is on Baffin's other side, he has to be the thin knight.

This clue also gives us the last man at the table, the knight who rode a white horse. And now that everyone is accounted for, we can see that Sir Coddle has to be the left-handed knight.

The last clue tells us that Sir Dollop sat to the right of the left-handed knight. We know that the fattest knight is sitting to the right of Sir Coddle, the left-handed knight, so the fattest knight is Sir Dollop. The clue says that Dollop sat next to Sir Mollix, and as the man to the right of Dollop has been established as the knight who rides a white horse, Mollix is the knight with the white horse.

1.

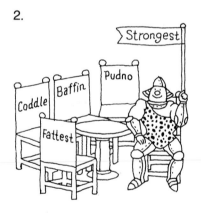

2.

4.

Answers

This leaves only one name unaccounted for—Sir Morgid, who is obviously the strongest knight.

"A nutty puzzle" (page 288)

To solve this puzzle, work backwards.

After making all his sales, Nicodemus had one dozen, or 12, nuts left. His third customer, the little girl, had bought one-third of what he had before that, so the twelve nuts were the other two-thirds. One-third is obviously six nuts. Thus, Nicodemus had 18 nuts (6 × 3 =18) before making the last sale.

Those 18 nuts were left *after* the second customer bought half of Nicodemus' nuts plus half a nut. Therefore, the 18 nuts must be half, *less one-half a nut*, of what Nicodemus had before his second sale. So, Nicodemus must have had 37 nuts—half of 37 is 18 1/2, plus a half is 19. The second customer bought 19 nuts, leaving Nicodemus with 18.

The 37 nuts were left from the first sale. The first customer bought half of Nicodemus' nuts, plus half a nut. So, the 37 nuts must be half, less half a nut, of what Nicodemus started with. Nicodemus must have started with 75 nuts. And the first customer bought 38—half of 75 is 37 1/2, plus a half is 38.

Answers

The lunch bunch (page 289)

The first clue tells us Mark had the same things Mary Jo did, except for an ice-cream sundae. So we know that one of the things Mary Jo had was an ice-cream sundae.

Clue 2 tells us Diana had what Brian did, plus a hamburger. So we know that Diana had a hamburger.

Clue 3 says that Gail had what Judy had, but without French fries. Obviously, Judy had French fries as part of her lunch.

Clue 4 tells us Mary Jo had what Judy had, but with pop instead of a milkshake. Thus, we now know that Mary Jo had French fries as Judy did, plus pop. We also found that Judy had a milkshake with her fries. And as clue 3 told us that Gail had what Judy did, but without fries, Gail had a milkshake, too.

Clue 5 says Brian had what Matt did, except that he did not have a hamburger. This tells us Matt had a hamburger. The very first clue told us Matt had the same things as Mary Jo, except for a sundae, so we can see that Matt had French fries and pop with his hamburger. And since he and Mary Jo had the same things, she must have had a hamburger, too. As for Brian, if he had what Matt did, without the hamburger, then he had French fries and pop. And if we go back to the second clue, we see that Diana had what Brian did—French fries and pop—plus a hamburger.

So, what the Lunch Bunch had was:
- Mary Jo: pop, hamburger, French fries, sundae
- Diana: pop, French fries, hamburger
- Judy: milkshake, French fries
- Gail: milkshake
- Matt: pop, French fries, hamburger
- Brian: pop, French fries

Fish stories (page 290)

1. The fish weighed 20 pounds (9 kilograms). Half its weight is 10 pounds (4.5 kgs), plus half again makes 20.

2. The fish's head is 4 inches (10 centimeters). The tail is as long as the head—4 inches—plus half the length of the body. And the body is as long as the head and tail together.

   Therefore, to find the length of the body, we add the 4-inch head, and the 4 known inches of the tail. This is 8 inches (20 cm), which has to be *half* the length of the body. So, the body is 16 inches (40 cm) long. The tail is 4 inches plus half the body length (8 inches) or 12 inches (30 cm) in all. So, the fish was 32 inches (80 cm) long.

   Head: 4 inches (10 cm)
   Tail: 12 inches (30 cm)
   Body: 16 inches (40 cm)
   Total: 32 inches (80 cm)

Illustration acknowledgments

The publishers of *Childcraft* gratefully acknowledge the courtesy of the following photographers, agencies, and organizations for illustrations in this volume. When all the illustrations for a sequence of pages are from a single source, the inclusive page numbers are given. Credits should be read from left to right, top to bottom, on their respective pages. All illustrations are the exclusive property of the publishers of *Childcraft* unless names are marked with an asterisk (*).

Cover:. Aristocrat and Standard Binding—Jan Jones; Yoshi Miyake; George Suyeoka
Heritage Binding—Bill Morrison; George Suyeoka; Jan Jones; George Suyeoka; Susan Lexa; Dennis Hockerman; Jan Jones; Diane Paterson; Yoshi Miyake

2–3:	Mr. Stobbs
8–9:	Mr. Stobbs
10–11:	Robert Byrd
12–13:	Jan Jones
14–15:	Dennis Hockerman
16:	Jan Jones
17–19:	Robert Byrd
20–21:	Jan Jones; Robert Byrd
22–23:	Jan Jones
24–25:	Robert Byrd
26–29:	Jan Jones
30:	Robert Byrd
31:	Dennis Hockerman; Denise Bohoy
32–33:	Robert Byrd; Dennis Hockerman
34–36:	Childcraft photos by Robert Frerck
37–38:	Robert Byrd; Jan Jones
39–40:	Jan Jones; Robert Byrd
41:	Jan Jones; Robert Byrd
42:	Jan Jones
44–45:	Mr. Stobbs
46:	Ronald LeHew
47–52:	Dennis Hockerman
53:	Ronald LeHew
54–55:	Dennis Hockerman; Ronald LeHew
56–57:	Dennis Hockerman; Ronald LeHew
58:	Dennis Hockerman; Ronald LeHew
59:	Dennis Hockerman
60–61:	Mr. Stobbs
62–63:	Robert Byrd; Bill Morrison
64–65:	Robert Byrd; Bill Morrison
66–67:	Christine di Monda; Robert Byrd
68–69:	Heidi Palmer
70–71:	Robert Byrd; Christine di Monda
72–73:	Heidi Palmer; Christine di Monda
75:	Heidi Palmer
77:	Bill Morrison
78–79:	Christine di Monda; Robert Byrd
80:	Christine di Monda
82–83:	Robert Byrd; Bill Morrison
84–85:	Christine di Monda; Robert Byrd
86–87:	Heidi Palmer
88–89:	Bill Morrison; Robert Byrd
90:	Heidi Palmer
92–94:	Robert Byrd
96–97:	Bill Morrison; Robert Byrd
98–99:	Mr. Stobbs
100–107:	Susan Lexa
108–109:	Mr. Stobbs
110–114:	Diane Paterson; George Suyeoka
115:	Diane Paterson
116:	George Suyeoka

116–117:	Diane Paterson; George Suyeoka
118–121:	George Suyeoka; Diane Paterson
122:	George Suyeoka; Diane Paterson
123–124:	Diane Paterson; George Suyeoka
125–126:	Diane Paterson
127:	George Suyeoka; Diane Paterson
128–133:	George Suyeoka
134–139:	Denise Bohoy; Diane Paterson
140–143:	Denise Bohoy
144–145:	Mr. Stobbs
146–147:	Yoshi Miyake; Kathy Clo
148–151:	Yoshi Miyake
152–153:	Kathy Clo
154–155:	Yoshi Miyake; Kathy Clo
156–157:	Yoshi Miyake
158:	Kathy Clo
159–160:	Yoshi Miyake
161:	Kathy Clo
162–163:	Yoshi Miyake
164–171:	Kathy Clo
172–173:	Mr. Stobbs
174–175:	Susan Lexa; Angela Adams
176–177:	Diane Paterson
178–179:	Angela Adams
180–181:	Susan Lexa
182–185:	Christine di Monda
186–187:	Susan Lexa
188–189:	Diane Paterson; Susan Lexa
190:	Christine di Monda
192–193:	Mr. Stobbs
194–201:	George Suyeoka
202–203:	Denise Bohoy; George Suyeoka
204–205:	Mr. Stobbs
206–207:	Robert Byrd; Christine di Monda
208–209:	Robert Byrd; Heidi Palmer
210–211:	Bill Morrison
212–213:	Christine di Monda
214–215:	Robert Byrd; Heidi Palmer
216–217:	Bill Morrison
218:	Christine di Monda
219–220:	Robert Byrd
221:	Heidi Palmer
222–223:	Christine di Monda
224–225:	Heidi Palmer
226–227:	Robert Byrd
228–231:	Bill Morrison
232–233:	Robert Byrd; Christine di Monda
237:	Heidi Palmer
238–239:	Robert Byrd
240–241:	Mr. Stobbs
242–243:	Susan Lexa; Kathy Clo
244–245:	Yoshi Miyake; Kathy Clo
246–247:	Yoshi Miyake
248–249:	Susan Lexa; Kathy Clo
250–251:	Susan Lexa
252–253:	Yoshi Miyake
254–255:	Kathy Clo; Denise Bohoy
256–257:	Yoshi Miyake
258:	Kathy Clo
259–260:	Susan Lexa
261:	Kathy Clo
262–263:	Yoshi Miyake
264:	Kathy Clo
266:	Yoshi Miyake
269:	Kathy Clo; Denise Bohoy
270:	Susan Lexa
272–273:	Mr. Stobbs
274–275:	Diane Paterson
276:	Ronald LeHew
277–279:	Diane Paterson
280–281:	George Suyeoka; Ronald LeHew
282–284:	George Suyeoka
285:	Ronald LeHew
286–287:	George Suyeoka
288–289:	Ronald LeHew; Diane Paterson
290:	Ronald LeHew
291–293:	Diane Paterson
294:	George Suyeoka
297:	Ronald LeHew
298–299:	George Suyeoka
301:	Ronald LeHew

Cyclo-teacher® The easy-to-use learning system

Features hundreds of cycles from seven valuable learning areas

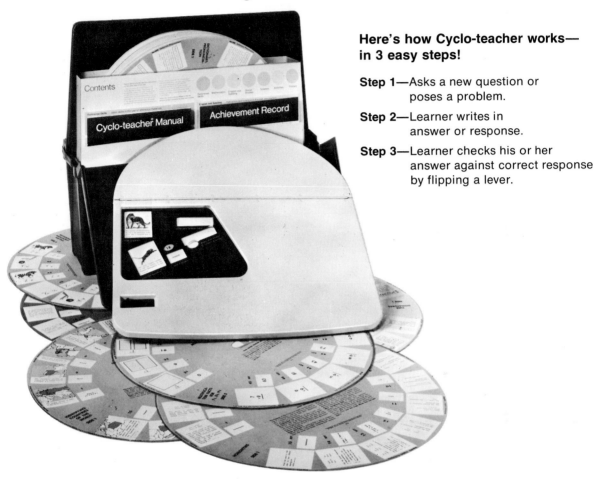

Here's how Cyclo-teacher works— in 3 easy steps!

Step 1—Asks a new question or poses a problem.

Step 2—Learner writes in answer or response.

Step 3—Learner checks his or her answer against correct response by flipping a lever.

Cyclo-teacher—the remarkable learning system based on the techniques of programmed instruction—comes right into your home to help stimulate and accelerate the learning of basic skills, concepts, and information. Housed in a specially designed file box are the Cyclo-teacher machine, Study Wheels, Answer Wheels, a Manual, a Contents and Instruction Card, and Achievement Record sheets.

Your child will find Cyclo-teacher to be a new and fascinating way to learn—much like playing a game. Only, Cyclo-teacher is much more than a game—it teaches new things

. . . reinforces learning . . . and challenges a youngster to go beyond!

Features hundreds of Study Cycles to meet the individual needs of students—your entire family—just as the *Childcraft Annual* is a valuable learning aid. And, best of all, lets you track your own progress—advance at your own pace! Cyclo-teacher is available by writing us at the address below:

The Childcraft Annual
Post Office Box 3822
Chicago, IL 60654

These beautiful bookstands—

specially designed to hold your entire program,
including *Childcraft Annuals*.

Height: 26-3/8''
with 4'' legs.
Width: 28-3/4''
Depth: 8-3/16''

Height: 8-3/4''
Width: 14-1/2''
Depth: 8''

Most parents like having a convenient place
to house their *Childcraft Annuals* and their
Childcraft library. A beautiful floor-model
bookstand—constructed of solid hardwood—is available in either walnut or
fruitwood finish.

You might prefer the attractive hardwood
table racks, also available in either walnut or
fruitwood finish. Let us know by writing us at
the following address:

The Childcraft Annual
Post Office Box 3822
Chicago, IL 60654